X06377

GW00390800

A 1926

THE NE~ ~~~DS

The Double-Dealer

THE NEW MERMAIDS

General Editors

BRIAN MORRIS

Principal, St Davids University College, Lampeter

BRIAN GIBBONS

Professor of English Literature, the University of Leeds

The Double-Dealer

WILLIAM CONGREVE

Edited by

J. C. ROSS

*Lecturer in English,
Massey University, New Zealand*

LONDON/ERNEST BENN LIMITED

NEW YORK/W. W. NORTON AND COMPANY INC.

First published 1981
by Ernest Benn Limited
25 New Street Square, Fleet Street, London EC4A 3JA

© *Ernest Benn Limited 1981*

Published in the United States of America by
W. W. Norton and Company Inc.
500 Fifth Avenue, New York, N.Y. 10036

Distributed in Canada by
The General Publishing Company Limited · Toronto

Printed in Great Britain

British Library Cataloguing in Publication Data

Congreve, William, *1670-1729*
 The double-dealer.—(The new mermaids)
 I. Title   II. Ross, John Clark   III. Series
822'.4   PR3364.D

ISBN 0-510-33504-7

CONTENTS

ACKNOWLEDGEMENTS

THE MODERN editions of Congreve's dramatic works that I have most often consulted are those by A. C. Ewald, Montague Summers, F. W. Bateson and Herbert Davis. Studies of Congreve and criticisms of this play by John C. Hodges, Emmet Avery, D. F. McKenzie, Peter Holland, Aubrey Williams, John Barnard, Harold Love and Maximilian Novak, among others, have been particularly valuable and enlightening. I have benefitted from the advice and help of David Mann, David Foxon, Paul Morgan and R. J. Roberts.

My thanks are due to the staff of the Bodleian Library, the Oxford University English Faculty Library, the British Library and the Massey University Library, and also of a number of American libraries that supplied me with microfilms. I am grateful to the Massey University Council for the grant of sabbatical leave that made this work possible, and also for a grant from the Social Sciences and Humanities Research Fund towards the cost of purchasing microfilms. I am thankful also to the General Editors of this series for the opportunity to undertake this project, and to the publisher Mr John Collis for his encouragement and meticulous attention to detail.

Very special gratitude is due to my wife Audrey for her partnership in the whole task, and in particular for preparing the typescript.

Massey University, N.Z.   J. C. ROSS
February 1981

LIST OF ABBREVIATIONS

Bateson Bateson, F.W., ed., *The Works of Congreve* (London, 1961)

Biographical Dictionary Highfill, Philip H., Jr., Birmin, Kalman A., Langhans, Edward A., edd., *A Bibliographical Dictionary of Actors, Actresses, Musicians, Dancers, Managers and Other Stage Personnel in London, 1660-1800* (Carbondale and Edwardsville, Illinois, 1973f., in progress)

Dryden, *Works* Swedenberg, H.T., Jr., general editor, *The Works of John Dryden* (Berkeley, California, 1956f., in progress)

Dryden, *Poems* Kinsley, J., ed., *The Poems of John Dryden*, 4 vols. (Oxford, 1959)

Ed. editorial emendation

ed. edited by

edn. edition

Ewald Ewald, Alex Charles, ed., *William Congreve [Plays]*, Mermaid series (London, 1887, etc.)

fig. figuratively

Holland Holland, Peter, *The Ornament of Action: Text and Performance in Restoration Comedy* (Cambridge, 1979)

Hume Hume, Robert D., *The Development of English Drama in the Late Seventeenth Century* (Oxford, 1976)

Loeb Loeb Classical Library series

The London Stage Lennep, W. Van, Avery, E. L., Scouten, A. H., Stone, G.W., and Hogan, C. B., edd., *The London Stage, 1660-1800*, 11 vols. (Carbondale, Illinois, 1965-8)

Lynch Lynch, Kathleen M., *The Social Mode of Restoration Comedy*, 2nd edn. (New York, 1965)

Macaulay Macaulay, Thomas Babington, *The History of England, from the Accession of James II*, etc., 5 vols. (London, 1848-61)

McKenzie McKenzie, D.F., *The London Book Trade in the Later Seventeenth Century*, Sandars Lectures (no place, 1976)

MLQ	*Modern Language Quarterly*
Morris	Morris, Brian, ed., *Mermaid Critical Commentaries: William Congreve* (London, 1970)
MP	*Modern Philology*
OED	*Oxford English Dictionary*
om.	omitted
POAS	Lord, George de F., *et al.*, edd., *Poems on Affairs of State: Augustan Satirical Verse, 1660-1714,* 7 vols. (New Haven, Connecticut, 1963-75)
Q1	first quarto (1694)
Q2	second quarto (1706)
S.D.	stage direction
SEL	*Studies in English Literature, 1500-1900*
Summers	Summers, Montague, ed., *The Complete Works of William Congreve,* 4 vols. (London, 1924)
Tilley	Tilley, Morris Palmer, *A Dictionary of the Proverbs in England in the Sixteenth and Seventeenth Centuries* (Ann Arbor, 1950)
transl.	translated by
W1	*Works* (1710) text
W2	*Works* (1719-20) text
Watson	Watson, George, ed., John Dryden, *Of Dramatic Poesy, and Other Critical Essays,* 2 vols. (London, 1962, etc.)
WCLD	Hodges, John C., ed., *William Congreve: Letters and Documents* (London, 1964)
WCM	Hodges, John C., *William Congreve the Man: a Biography from New Sources,* MLA Publications, General Series, XI (New York, 1941)
Williams	Williams, Aubrey, *An Approach to Congreve* (New Haven and London, 1979)

Citations from Lee's plays are from *The Works of Nathaniel Lee,* edd. Stroup, Thomas B., and Cooke, Arthur L., 2 vols. (Metuchen, New Jersey, 1968); and from Wycherley's, from *The Plays of William Wycherley,* ed. Friedman, Arthur (Oxford, 1979)

INTRODUCTION

THE AUTHOR

WILLIAM CONGREVE was born in January 1670, as the only son of the second son of a landed gentleman, Richard Congreve of Stretton Hall, in Staffordshire.[1] His birthplace was Bardsey Grange, within the Yorkshire estate of a wealthy uncle. So it was that the chances of birth endowed him with the class standing and family connections of a gentleman, while denying him a gentleman's private income.

In 1674 his father obtained a commission as a lieutenant in the army in Ireland. The family moved first to the seaport of Youghal, then in 1678 to Carrickfergus, and in 1681 to Kilkenny. It seems likely that Lieutenant Congreve was associated with the establishment of the Boyles, the Earls of Cork and Burlington, in some capacity that made him not wholly dependent on his unreliable military pay. After the Battle of the Boyne in October 1690 he became the chief agent for administering the Earl's Irish estates.

William's education evidently began at the Free School in Youghal, and it progressed through the highly-regarded preparatory school in Kilkenny to Trinity College, Dublin. The Trinity records show him working particularly diligently in Greek, but missing lectures in some less favoured subjects. And he probably slipped out often to see plays at the Smock Alley Theatre.

Following the Revolution of December 1688 the Congreves moved to England; and on 17 March 1691, when his father was once again in a position back in Ireland to support him, William was admitted as a student of the law at the Middle Temple in London. A general familiarity with the legal system was to be put to good use in his plays and in his various later employments; yet as a templar he was not obliged to spend much time studying, and devoted himself to writing, playgoing and enjoying the company of men of wit and letters.

His first literary works to be published were the short novel *Incognita*, which appeared in February 1692 (though possibly written while still at Trinity), and some poetry, mainly translations of the classics. The most important was his contribution to the *Satires* of Juvenal and Persius, edited by John Dryden, issued in

---

[1] This information is drawn mainly from John C. Hodges, *William Congreve: Letters and Documents* (London, 1964).

October.[2] Congreve provided the eleventh satire of Juvenal, and complimentary verses prefaced to Dryden's translations of Persius.

The central idea of this satire, translated only a few months before he launched into writing *The Double-Dealer,* is crucial to this play and (in the guise of marriage) to all his later dramatic work. It is the ideal of true companionship, and (in Novak's words) 'profound understanding . . . between two people of wit and sensibility,' sustained in the face of a world of knavery, folly, debauchery and vulgar ostentation.

Congreve's own natural gift for forming such relationships is demonstrated through his letters and the testimony of his friends. He would later write of his own love and admiration for Dryden, and in 1704 confide to Joseph Keally that 'the greatest trial' of his philosophy was 'that I know not how to have the few people that I love as near me as I want.'[3] His own increasing preference was for few rather than many friendships; nonetheless he became widely regarded as a man of unusual honesty and good-nature, and in an era of bitter factional strife made himself no enemies.

Of special importance was the friendship of John Dryden, who wrote to Jacob Tonson on 30 August 1693, 'I am Mr. Congreve's true Lover and desire you to tell him, how kindly I take his often Remembrances of me: I wish him all prosperity; and hope I shall never lose his Affection' (*WCLD,* p. 93). The old poet quickly developed a great esteem for the 'Excellent Parts' of the young novice, as a scholar, translator and poet, and when in 1692 Congreve showed him the manuscript of a comedy, *The Old Bachelor,* on which he had been working over the past few years,

> [he] sayd he never saw such a first play in his life, but the Author not being acquainted with the stage or the town, it wou'd be pity to have it miscarry for want of a little Assistance: the stuff was rich indeed, it wanted only the fashionable cutt of the town. To help that Mr Dryden, Mr Arthur Manwayring, and Mr Southerne red it with great care, and Mr Dryden putt it in the order it was playd.[4]

The production at the Drury Lane Theatre benefitted from an extended rehearsal period, and when at last the première came in March 1693 it scored a prodigious success, with an initial run of

---

[2] *The Satires of Decimus Junius Juvenalis* [translated by Dryden *et al.,* and] *of Aulus Persius Flaccus* [translated by Dryden] was dated '1693' but advertised as published in *The London Gazette* of 24-7 October 1692.

[3] Dedicatory epistle, Dryden, *The Dramatick Works* (1717-19); letter to Keally, 12 February 1704 (*WCLD,* pp. 124-9, 28).

[4] Dedicatory epistle, *Examen Poeticum* (1693); reminiscences of Thomas Southerne (1736) (*WCLD,* pp. 89-90, 151).

fourteen days; and Congreve at once became publicly recognized as one of the best and certainly the most promising of the comic dramatists of the day. Among the complimentary verses printed with the play are Thomas Southerne's, saluting him as the rightful successor to Dryden as England's leading writer: '*Heir to his Merit, be in Fame his Son.*'

Apart from the superior artistry of its prose and the brilliant vitality of its characters, *The Old Bachelor* was not strikingly different from some comedies of the preceding few years, by Southerne, Shadwell or Mountfort. His next play, *The Double-Dealer*, was a venture into a new territory of serio-comic tone and neo-classical structure. Other dramatists had already been writing comedies quite seriously satiric in tone, each in his own way, and Congreve's seriousness had nothing of the tearful repentance of Shadwell's *The Scowrers* (1690), indeed made mock of it in Lady Touchwood's pretended reformation (IV,vi), or of the Juvenalian sense of pervasive rancidness of Otway's *The Atheist* (1684) or Southerne's *The Wives' Excuse* (1691). In his interest in marriages going wrong he followed Southerne. In his quest for a more elevated tone he was in line with Dryden's lifelong programme for comedy that would offer 'a nobler pleasure'. In these respects the play was an experiment in a mode that, with a difference, would have its fullest expression in *The Way of the World*.

The Double-Dealer evidently had its first performance in early November 1693.[5] After the precocious triumph accorded 'not long since' to what its author felt to be 'a very imperfect comedy,' the public reception of this more ambitious effort was grievously disappointing. An unidentified contemporary observed that 'It has fared with that play, as it generally does with beauties officiously cried up: the mighty expectation which was raised of it made it sink, even beneath its own merit.'[6] By 12 December it 'has been acted Eight times,' and 'gets ground daily'; so it was by no means an outright failure.[7] What was however worse, it was 'unreasonably overrun' by 'boisterous Cavils.'[8] Dryden wrote in December that,

---

[5] See the section on 'Stage History.' It was mentioned as forthcoming in *The Gentleman's Journal* for February 1693 (p. 61), and probably went into rehearsal in September.

[6] Letter, 22 March 1694, cited in *The London Stage*, I, 433.

[7] Letter, Dryden to Walsh, 12 December 1693 (*WCLD*, pp. 95-6).

[8] Colley Cibber, epistle 'To the Reader,' *Ximena; or the Heroic Daughter* (1719), p. xx.

His Double-Dealer is much censurd by the greater part of the Town: and is defended onely by the best Judges ... The women thinke he has exposd their Bitchery too much; and the Gentlemen, are offended with him; for the discovery of their follyes: and the way of their Intrigues, under the notion of Friendship to their Ladyes Husbands.[9]

It may be, equally, that given the increasing concern of the ladies in the audience with sexual propriety, they 'objected to *what* was shown; the gentlemen of the pit objected to the negative *way* it was shown,' in a morally serious satire (Hume, p. 390). Then again, in the fashioning of his play Congreve had made few concessions to popular taste; but the support he had hoped for from more sophisticated playgoers proved to be weaker than the chorus of hostile criticisms that arose.

Congreve expressed his hurt and indignation in his dedicatory epistle, and again in Act I of his next play, where Jeremy and Scandal combine to describe the wretchedness of the situation of any man who sets out to make a living or a reputation as a playwright. The comment was made that he 'lashed' his critics in the epistle 'in so defying or hectoring a style, that it was counted rude even by his best friends; so that 'tis generally thought he has done his business, and lost himself . . .' The more 'hectoring' passages were dropped when the play was reprinted; it is indicative of its limited popularity that this second edition did not appear till 1706, whereas five editions of *The Old Bachelor* had been issued in 1693, and two more in the following year.

It may be apropos that during 1693 he was suffering from painful digestive troubles, spending part of the summer at Tunbridge Wells and at Epsom, to take the water in the hope of getting relief. His friend Jonathan Swift remarks that it was Congreve's 'misfortune to squander away a very good constitution in his younger days,' by excessively heavy eating and drinking.[10] Henceforth he would have substantial periods of illness, and in addition he developed cataracts in his eyes, that were removed in due course but which left his sight weakened.

London at this time possessed only one theatre company and every playwright who hoped for success had to try to custombuild his plays to suit the particular strengths of its actors and actresses. Congreve became an expert observer and exploiter of the stage-personalities and talents of these people, most of all the young leading actress Anne Bracegirdle, with whom he was in love for many years. All of

---

[9] See Note 7.
[10] Letter to Alexander Pope, 13 February 1729 (*WCLD*, p. 240).

his main heroine roles were written for her. As Colley Cibber remarks, Congreve and Rowe 'when they gave her a Lover, in a play, seem'd palpably to plead their own Passions'.[11]

By late 1694 financial disputes with the managers of the United Company had become so bitter that the main body of the actors determined to split off and form a new company. On 30 April 1695 they opened in a small converted tennis court in Lincoln's Inn Fields, with Congreve's latest comedy, *Love for Love.* Its own great merits, public sympathy for the new company, and the best efforts of a very fine group of actors combined to make it a phenomenal success. And his one tragedy, *The Mourning Bride,* which opened on 27 February 1697, achieved an even greater triumph.

During the 1690s rumblings were growing against the indecency of the 'hard' comedies, and April 1698 saw the publication of the most effective of the attacks on the contemporary theatre, Jeremy Collier's *A Short View of the Immorality and Profaneness of the English Stage.* It gave particular prominence to complaints against recent plays by Congreve and Sir John Vanbrugh. *The Double-Dealer* received Collier's attention on several grounds: 'jesting at Scripture' and Christianity (for example, in naming a coachman Jehu, and in Cynthia's comment on marriage making man and wife one flesh but still two fools); its debased, 'unimproving' view of society ('There are but Four Ladies in this Play and three of the biggest of them are Whores'); irreverent treatment of the clergy, in the person of Chaplain Saygrace; and the profane or obscene character of a number of phrases and exclamations. Congreve among others made a reply to him, with *Amendments of Mr Collier's False and Imperfect Citations, &c.* (1698), for the most part very reasonably. But Collier was a shrewd and relentlessly persistent controversialist, and the general reaction of public opinion was that Collier's moral objections were simply too strong to be answered.[12]

The great stir created by this affair accelerated the shift in the moral climate in which the theatres operated, both in public attitudes towards them, and in the audiences' tendency to protest noisily about anything they found objectionable. It focussed attention on those passages in plays that Collier himself had complained about. Narcissus Luttrell records on 5 May 1698 that at the Quarter Sessions the Grand Jury of Middlesex 'did not only present the playhouses, but also Mr. Congreve, for writing the

[11] *An Apology for the Life of Colley Cibber,* ed. B.R.S. Fone (Ann Arbor, 1968), p. 98.
[12] Sister Rose Anthony, *The Jeremy Collier Stage Controversy, 1698-1726* (Milwaukee, Wisconsin, 1937), *passim.*

WILLIAM CONGREVE

Double-Dealer; Durfey for Don Quixot; and Tonson and Brisco, booksellers, for printing them.'[13] A royal order was made on 18 February 1699 that the theatres should 'not hereafter presume to Act anything in any Play, contrary to Religion or good Manners'; and the play-bill advertising a revival of *The Double-Dealer* on 4 March specified 'with Severall Expressions omitted.'[14]

Congreve completed one more comedy, his masterpiece *The Way of the World*, which was performed in March 1700 with no more than moderate success. Then as a matter of conscious decision he turned away from writing stage-plays, at the age of thirty, since he refused to 'prostitute his muse to the lower taste of the town' and 'the London audience would not accept the type of high comedy that now satisfied his artistic sense' (*WCM*, p. 70). This noble resolve seems to have failed only once, when in early 1704 he collaborated with Vanbrugh and William Walsh in dashing off *Squire Trelooby*, an adaptation of a Molière farce; otherwise his later literary work included a masque, an opera libretto, occasional verse, and other miscellaneous writing. For several years, 1703-05, he was strenuously involved in the building of a new theatre in the Haymarket and in the day-to-day organisation of Betterton's acting company that moved into it; but its poor acoustics and unsuitable location doomed this costly venture to failure.

Thereafter he devoted himself to the very limited duties of his public offices, to the society of his friends, which included his membership of the influential Kit-Cat Club, a congerie of writers and Whig politicians, and to his relationship with Henrietta, wife of the Earl of Godolphin, and by inheritance the second Duchess of Marlborough. He died on 19 January 1729, and was buried with honour in Westminster Abbey.

SOURCES

Congreve's statement in his dedicatory epistle, that 'to that moral I invented the fable, and do not know that I have borrowed one hint of it anywhere,' can be given general credence. While the plot is essentially original, he has nonetheless drawn his materials primarily from other plays, and in particular from those prominent in the theatrical repertory of 1691-3. *The Double-Dealer* is a conspicuously 'literary'

---

[13] *A Brief Relation*, IV, 376. McKenzie reprints the presentation (p. 41).
[14] *The London Gazette*, 27 February 1699; cf. *WCLD*, pp. 102-3.

work; and some of these uses of other plays were manifestly intended
to be recognized, by sophisticated playgoers, as ironic allusions to
their original contexts, and to the performances of well-known actors
and actresses.

The composition of the United Company, and the established
'lines' of its leading members, in 1693, would in themselves have
been significant influences (see Holland, pp. 139-60). In particular,
its lack of a first-class performer of witty fine gentleman roles,
following the murder of Mountfort in the previous December, must
have helped to encourage Congreve to design his most demanding
male role, Maskwell, for the old master Thomas Betterton. In the
comedies of the last decade he had created a series of increasingly less
attractive rakes, as cynical manipulators (Holland, p. 81). The male
romantic lead, Mellefont, and his friend Careless, were made not too
demanding for the weaker actors Williams and Verbruggen; and the
false-wit role of Brisk was developed for George Powell. The
established triangle of Betterton—Elizabeth Barry—Anne Bracegirdle (as hero, savagely passionate female lead, and gentle heroine) was
built in through the explicit and implicit relationships of Maskwell,
Lady Touchwood and Cynthia.

John Dryden's lineage of the play in his complimentary verses
mentions Jonson, Fletcher, Etherege, Southerne and Wycherley. To
these may be added Terence, Shakespeare, Nathaniel Lee, Thomas
Shadwell, Thomas Durfey, William Mountfort and Thomas
Wright. (A hostile commentator described Congreve's plays, aptly
but unfairly, as 'little Compounds of the whole Body of Scribblers.'[15])

Terence's comedies, and most notably the Heautontimorumenos,
are used not as a source but as a precedent and model for basically
serious comedy in which the main action is one of deception and
gulling. The second epigraph added in Q2 (1706) calls attention to
the fact that Terence's Syrus and Congreve's Maskwell both use the
trick of telling the truth to more effectively deceive.[16] Yet it had also
been recommended to Gracian's courtier: 'when . . . his Artifice is
known,' the expert 'refines his dissimulation, making use of truth
itself to deceive by,' etc.[17] Maskwell's position as a dependant in the
Touchwood household is comparable to that of Syrus, the cunning

---

[15] Anon., *Animadversions on Mr. Congreve's Late Answer to Mr. Collier* (1698), p. 7.
[16] The first epigraph also implicitly alludes to this play: 'Yet at times even comedy
raises her voice' is followed by 'And an angry Chremes storms in swelling tones' (*Ars
Poetica*, 93-4 [Loeb]).
[17] Balthazar Gracian, *The Courtier's Manual Oracle, or the Art of Prudence* (1685), p.
10.

slave, but the purposes of his trickery are altogether more self-seeking and destructive.

More obviously important, as the title implies, is the affinity with Wycherley's *The Plain Dealer* (1676). This also implies reversal: the greatest dramatic interest centres not on the plain-dealing Mellefont, but on the double-dealing Maskwell. Charles Gildon early recognized the latter as 'an Image of *Vernish*,' the trusted scoundrel who conspires to rob his friend of his wealth and tries to possess his girl.[18] Maskwell also has affinities with the Machiavellian 'statesmen' of Restoration tragedy, such as Cassander in *The Rival Queens*.

Congreve's play resembles Wycherley's in the serious, even melodramatic, quality of its main action, in its emphasis on satire, and in its 'invention', that is, the structure of relationships of its central characters. Mellefont corresponds to Manly, as the credulous but on the whole sympathetic figure who is deceived for much of the play by a scheming woman (Lady Touchwood, Olivia) and a treacherous, false friend, but preserved from disaster through the help of a true friend (Careless, Freeman) and of the girl who loves him (Cynthia, Fidelia).

As far as the lesser characters were concerned. Thomas Davies commented that 'Brisk's pertness is not unlike the petulance of Novel in the *Plain Dealer*, and Lord Froth's solemnity is an improvement of Lord Plausible's starch civility.'[19] As a would-be wit, Brisk also has a strong family resemblance to Sparkish in Wycherley's *The Country-Wife* (1675), who begins his feeble joke in I,i (271f.) with 'Nay then, since you are so brisk and provoke me, take what follows.'

The sequences in Act III (501-518, 522-540), in which Brisk and the Froths make fun of Lady Whiffler and other absent acquaintances, are parallel to the scandal session in Wycherley's Act II, scene i (lines 154-385), in which Olivia, Plausible and Novel gossip about the guests who had been at Lady Autumn's dinner (and which in its turn was suggested by Molière's *Le Misanthrope*, II,iv). Cynthia plays a similar role here to Eliza, as the woman-of-sense commentator. Two elements not carried across are Olivia's hypocrisy in denying that she ever does rail at anyone, and the competitive, vicious nature of the raillery.

Further aspects in which Wycherley's play served as a stimulus were: the use, in the epilogue, of the image of the play in the theatre as a defendant in a court of law; the notion of 'the Man of most Wit

---

[18] *The Lives and Characters of the English Dramatick Poets,* etc. (1699), p. 22. John Wilcox rejects any resemblance of Maskwell to Tartuffe, or any other debt to Molière, in *The Relation of Molière to Restoration Comedy* (New York, 1938), p. 160.
[19] *Dramatic Miscellanies,* etc. (1783-4), III, 320, Cf. I,i.30-4 and note.

... having no vanity in showing it everywhere' (V,ii. 197-9); and 'the shadowing of comedy by the heroic', in casting, values and diction (Holland, p. 184).

In its subsidiary action *The Double-Dealer* draws instead for its invention upon Shadwell's *Epsom Wells* (1672), in which the three married couples, the genteel Woodlys and the citizen Biskets and Fribbles, anticipate at a lower social level the Touchwoods, Plyants and Froths. The fiery Mrs Woodly's pursuit of younger men leads to compromising situations and eventual separation. Mr. Bisket is ludicrously subservient to his wife, whereas the Fribbles make a display of mutual fondness. The citizen husbands both desire children, and are cuckolded in the course of the play, a fact they discover yet accept.

Lady Plyant and Sir Paul belong to the same character-formulae as Lady Cockwoud and Sir Oliver, in George Etherege's *She Would if She Could* (1668), as the lustful but self-declaredly prudish married woman, who believes herself attractive to young men (by 1693, a favourite line of Mrs Leigh), and her humour-butt, over-uxorious husband.[20] Sir Oliver's penitential suit doubtless provided a hint for the swaddling of Sir Paul. The similarity of surnames calls attention to the parallels that also exist between the Cockwouds and Lord and Lady Touchwood, in their capacities as heavy parents, and barrier-figures to the loves of the young.[21] Lady Cockwoud's counter-accusations after she has been found in compromising situations with one or other of the young men, including a seemingly reluctant declaration that Courtall had tried to force her (IV,i. 74-94), have comic and serious equivalents in the accusations that Lady Plyant and Lady Touchwood make against Mellefont.

The put-upon, uxorious husband, a traditional type who was usually a citizen, like Fondlewife in *The Old Bachelor* (see Lynch, pp. 190-1), appeared with an exalted social status as Lord Malepert in Thomas Southerne's *The Maid's Last Prayer* (February 1693). Both he and Fondlewife discover their wives in suspicious circumstances with young rakes, and let themselves be persuaded into wilfully blinding themselves to intolerable truths. The actor Thomas Doggett created both roles, as well as Sir Paul, and seems to have made a speciality of this routine. Lord Malepert's inane pride in his wife's accomplishments ('you must know my Wife understands State

---

[20] *She Would if She Could* was reprinted in 1693, so may have been revived in the 1692-3 season (*The London Stage*, I, 413); if so, Sir Oliver may well have been played then by Doggett, as in 1702-3 (*Biographical Dictionary*, IV, 447).

[21] 'Lord Touchwood's name and temper were perhaps suggested by Touchwood in Brome's *The Sparagus Garden*' (Lynch, p. 190n.).

Affairs to a Miracle'—p. 5) prefigured Sir Paul's, while his vapid egotism and use of the exclamation 'O Jesu' contributed to the resources of the aristocratic fop, from which Congreve developed Lord Froth.

Lady Froth as a female fop with cultural pretensions had antecedents in Mrs Fantast in Shadwell's *Bury Fair* (1689) and the three ladies in Thomas Wright's *The Female Virtuosos* (April 1693); but she goes far beyond them as the earliest dramatic portrayal of an authoress. 'So far as is known, Congreve intended his satire on her to be impersonal and to bear no direct relation to any contemporary woman writer.'[22] The sequence in Act III in which Brisk admires Lady Froth's poetry amusingly reverses a situation in Wright's play (II,i; pp. 16-18), itself derived from Molière's *Les Femmes Savantes*, III,ii, in which three ladies ridiculously over-praise verses recited by a masculine scribbler.

Lady Touchwood has been said to greatly resemble Bacha in Fletcher's *Cupid's Revenge* (c. 1615); and the sequence in Act IV scene ii of that play, in which Bacha 'cunningly inflames the old duke' Leontius, her husband, by alleging that his son by an earlier marriage has tried to rape her, has been proposed as a source for the episode in which Lady Touchwood arouses her husband against Mellefont, in Act III.[23] The sequences are undeniably parallel, but Congreve's equally has something in common with Iago's arousing of the suspicions of Othello, and the comic allegations of Lady Cockwould. The borrowing is not proven. Lady Touchwood's affinities are more closely with the lustful villainesses of Restoration tragedy, and the termagant wives and mistresses of the comedy.

Two plays to which allusions are strikingly ostentatious are *Othello*, and Lee's *The Rival Queens* (1677). The former appears mainly in demands for 'ocular proof' or, in a parody of Rymer, 'mathemacular demonstration'. The use of Lee's play was far more pervasive. The original triangle of Hart—Rebecca Marshall—Elizabeth Boutell, for whom the roles of Alexander, Roxana and Statira had been composed, had long been succeeded by Better-

---

[22] Jean Gagen, *The New Woman: her Emergence in English Drama, 1660-1730* (New York, 1954), p. 71,72-4; cf. Myra Reynolds, *The Learned Lady in England 1650-1760*, Vassar semi-centennial series (Boston and New York, 1920), pp. 380-6.

[23] Davies, III, 320; Summers, II, 3. See *The Dramatic Works in the Beaumont and Fletcher Canon*, general editor F. Bowers (Cambridge, 1966-79), II, 391-2. John Harold Wilson, *The Influence of Beaumont and Fletcher on Restoration Drama* (Columbus, Ohio, 1928), pp. 65-6, perceives *Cupid's Revenge* as the major source for Congreve's plot; but the resemblance is, at most, tangential.

ton—Mrs Barry—Mrs Bracegirdle (Maskwell, Lady Touchwood and Cynthia).[24] Lady Touchwood in moments of fury repeatedly echoes the words of Roxana; and comically inappropriate characters, Brisk and Sir Paul, briefly posture as the towering figure of Alexander the Great.[25] To an extent that has not been recognized, yet would be tedious to document, Congreve's diction in the more serious parts of *The Double-Dealer* is permeated by that of *The Rival Queens,* and of other tragedies of Nathaniel Lee.

THE PLAY

> The plot is extremely intricate, and exacts from the spectator very deep attention; without it, he will not be able to see how it is unravelled in the catastrophe.[26]

Thomas Davies, writing from a long-standing familiarity with the play in the eighteenth century theatre, points to one side of its central paradox: that despite its avowedly rigorous commitment to classical principles of construction, it pursues the highly unclassical practices of creating surprise by violating generated expectations, and violently shifting in tone and perspective. It demands alertness, not just because the plot is intricate, but also because 'the audience is deliberately confused, refused the security of expectation of what a play ought to do' (Holland, p. 205). Congreve's second comedy is radically ambitious and experimental, along several diverging paths.

The effect of the Horatian epigraph, together with the claim in the dedicatory epistle that 'the mechanical part' of the play is 'perfect' ('regular' in Q2), is to assert that *The Double-Dealer* complies with the requirements for comedy as laid down by both ancient and more recent classical critics. Yet if the play is arguably 'regular,' by accepted standards, it is less clear that it is the 'true . . . comedy' that its author tried to write.

The epigraph 'Yet at times even comedy raises her voice,' in its original context came within a discussion of generic and stylistic decorum: 'Let each style keep the becoming place allotted to it. Yet . . .' Horace accepted nonetheless the legitimacy of the occasional

---

[24] Cf. Eric Rothstein, *Restoration Tragedy: Form and the Process of Change* (Madison, 1967), pp. 139-44; Holland, pp. 217-8.

[25] Cf. P.F. Vernon: 'Within a short period *The Rival Queens* attained the status of a popular, but somewhat antiquated, classic.' Deliberate echoes are frequent, 'but by the 1690s most references are humorous.' He notices Sir Paul's quotation. (Introduction to the Regents edition [1970], pp. xvi-xvii.)

[26] *Dramatic Miscellanies,* III, 320.

emergence within a comedy of intensely passionate, serious and elevated speeches, akin to those of tragedy, provided they were appropriate to character and situation. And André Dacier's comment on this line, in a standard critical work of the time (referred to in the play) allowed that a more heightened, sublime mode of speech might be introduced not only for moments of rage, but to express any strong passion, even joy.[27] Congreve is invoking the authority of Horace and, by implication, the precedent of Terence's comedies (one of which Horace refers to in the following line, see p. xv), to justify his thrusting outward, or actual violation, of the generic boundaries of comedy, by introducing into his main action sequences that approach both the intense passions and the heightened diction of contemporary tragedy. Comparisons can be made with certain of the tragicomedies of John Dryden (e.g. *The Spanish Friar*) in which the high action was largely serious yet turned out happily, and the low action comic.

The author's declaration that he has 'preserved' the three unities 'to the utmost severity' is not in the strictest sense correct. He complies with them to the generally accepted degree: a time-span of within twenty-four hours, a few places reasonably close to each other, and the pre-eminence of one action, to which lesser actions are related.[28] However the interpretations with which Congreve has tried to comply are far narrower. He has not quite managed to do so, and the play would have suffered badly theatrically if he had placed too high a priority on this. To have made the statement as it stood in the first quarto, 'The SCENE, A Gallery in the Lord *Touchwood*'s House,' literally true, could only have been achieved by reducing the episode in Lady Touchwood's bed-chamber, at the end of Act IV, either to 'noises off' and messenger report, or to a thoroughly implausible intrusion of part of its action out on to the gallery. Either way would have meant a grievous sacrifice of 'beauties' and dramatic values at a point where the play needed an effective crisis. As it is, this brief 'private' scene draws added power and symbolic value from its uniqueness.

Similarly, the statement in Q1 that 'The Time' is 'from Five o'Clock to Eight in the Evening' asserts that the fictive time is equal to the playing-time, and indeed more or less identical with the time of the performance in the Restoration theatre. Here there is an element of *trompe l'oeil*: in the text five references in Acts III and IV to the hour eight o'clock encourage us, despite our growing awareness

[27] *Ars Poetica*, 93, 92 (Loeb). Dacier, *Les Œuvres d'Horace*, etc., 2nd edn. (Paris, 1691), X, 142-3.
[28] Cf. Dryden, *Essay of Dramatic Poesy* (Watson, I, 29-30, 63-4).

of Maskwell's true intentions, to anticipate a decisive catastrophe at this time. Instead the events in the bed-chamber multiply the complications, in Jonsonian fashion, and Act V requires approximately one further hour. Maskwell in V, iii. 36-37 tells Mellefont 'meet me in half an hour, yonder in my lady's dressing-room,' and the resultant meetings bring about the true catastrophe. The audience would simply be aware, like Lord Froth, that the final events occur at some time 'past eight' (V,v. 2), as if the clock had accelerated towards eight o'clock and then stopped, leaving them to unfold in a kind of temporal limbo. The time required for events off-stage between the acts would have corresponded, ostensibly, with the duration of the act-intervals, in which the Restoration audience was entertained with music.[29]

Once again, the dramatist claims he has complied with the most stringent version of the unity of action, by making his plot 'single'; this implies that Brisk's cuckolding intrigue with Lady Froth, and Careless's with Lady Plyant, are not intended to be regarded as minor plots at all, but simply as business, the goings-on of the social milieu in relation to which the plot functions and is to be understood. Alternatively the Careless/Plyant strand may be regarded as an aspect of the central plot. But clearly the minor characters' activities are by no means so skilfully woven into a single complex action as in *Love for Love* or *The Way of the World*.

Even allowing that Congreve's proclaimed compliance involves an element of disingenuousness, a conscious manipulation of the reader, the extremely tight limits within which his play works are vital to its nature. They are exceptional for the era, and very difficult to handle with an appearance of naturalness. From the frequent and precise references to time, and to where characters are, or are going, and why, one may glimpse (and reconstruct) a schema in which, as in a detective-story play like Agatha Christie's *The Mousetrap*, the whereabouts of almost every character, in the house or the garden, at crucial times, has been exactly charted. As Peter Holland observes, the narrow time-scheme 'produces in the play an incredible claustrophobic intensity,' and an effect of 'excessive naturalism' (pp. 220-1).

The virtually constant presence of the ornate gallery setting is likewise claustrophobic. 'No previous Restoration comedy had stayed so firmly in one place, had excluded the outside world so completely' (Holland, p. 221). It serves to symbolise the closed nature of the upper class society we observe, and also, in its elegance, the

---

[29] In II, 378-9, Maskwell tells Mellefont 'be here in this gallery an hour hence'; and the rendezvous occurs about 10 minutes into Act III.

privilege, wealth and status which accompany the possession of this great house, that ultimately the conflict is about. One hears further of a bewildering maze of rooms, stairs and back-passages, which give power to those like Maskwell who know them all. Only convention, in the absence of evidence to the contrary, and slight hints like the reference to Sappho's 'chair,' indicate that the house is in the environs of London. The gallery setting thus also takes on a limbo-esque quality, 'real and unreal at the same time' (Holland, p. 221); and this is enhanced by the stagey quality of the long soliloquies (emphatically placed as they are), the end-of-act tags, and the more artificially heightened speeches.

Other features of classical regularity include the preservation of *liaison des scènes*, which has been largely though not completely achieved.[30]

That the dramatist was actively conscious of neoclassical critical writings at this time is evidenced not merely by his implicit use of Hédelin and Dryden in his dedicatory epistle. The play's own critical self-consciousness is amusingly revealed in Brisk's questioning Lady Froth in Act III as to whether she has read Rapin, Le Bossu and André Dacier. She has.

*   *   *   *

As a 'true comedy' the play is committed to satirical instruction by negative example. Not only is there incidental display of a variety of follies; we are told that the central plot is designed to illustrate a moral. What exactly it does demonstrate may be argued about; but Congreve leaves us in no doubt that his intended moral is expressed in Lord Touchwood's closing words: that the treacherous person is inevitably destroyed by his own treachery. The play is not outwardly political; yet treachery (or as those opposed to the regime would call it, Jacobite loyalty) was an intensely relevant political issue amid fears of invasion, subversion and uprising in 1692-3.[31] Some later historians describe Marlborough as one of the arch double-dealers of the time; but there is no clear trace in the play of personal satire.[32]

In the moral the fate of 'secret villainy' is to be like that of Volpone's 'mischiefs,' which 'feed/Like beasts till they be fat and then they bleed.' One of the key images in the play, of the viper in the bosom, is now used to represent Maskwell's treachery as a viper

[30] Cf. Gunnar Sorelius, *'The Giant Race before the Flood': Pre-Restoration Drama on the Stage and in the Criticism of the Restoration* (Uppsala, 1966), pp. 89-90.

[31] See Longer Notes, No. 1.

[32] E.g. George M. Thomson, *The First Churchill* (London, 1979), pp. 75, 84.

that is emerging and will destroy him, by a process of natural law. It becomes then essential that Maskwell be seen to be defeated not primarily through Mellefont's or anyone else's initiatives, but through the consequence of his own machinations. The dynamic of the central action thus becomes that of Jonsonian 'punitive comedy.'[33] And as the moral governs the plot, so the central plot in its turn takes on a 'set-piece' quality, and to a large degree governs the characterization of the people involved in it.[34]

As Irving Wardle has said, 'The Double-Dealer is a double play, combining the usual provisional morality of folly and ill-breeding' of Restoration comedy 'with a fixed morality based on the sense of evil.'[35] In practice the double valuation is all-pervasive. The Froths, the Plyants and Brisk belong firmly in the world normally portrayed by Restoration social comedy; yet their shallow egotism and follies reveal the vulnerability of this realm to the corruptions of serious evil. In the central plot the dynamics and valuations of serious 'punitive comedy' are juxtaposed with the very different expectations and valuations that the social comedy mode generates.

Conventionally the central and normative male figure in the Restoration social comedy was the young rake-wit, and the main action his eventually successful courting of the heroine. The pattern was susceptible of great variation, in particular, in the contrast between a rake-hero and a romantic lead (as reproduced by, e.g., Dorimant and Young Bellair in Etherege's The Man of Mode): and in the 1680s the predatory rake was becoming less attractive. Nonetheless the pattern, and the audience expectations it generated, remained extremely potent.

What has happened in The Double-Dealer is that the intriguing rake is presented as the 'villain,' the barrier-figure and rival to the love of the romantic lead Mellefont. And Maskwell as a hybrid character carries not only the moral ambivalence of the rake-hero, unscrupulously hunting after sex and a fortune; he also brings with him the double valuation of the Jonsonian rogue, at once hero and villain.

In this play the action begins where the typical social comedy ended: the courting is completed and the rather serious romantic couple,

---

[33] Cf. Brian Corman, ' "The Mixed Way of Comedy": Congreve's The Double-Dealer,' MP, LXXI (1974), 356-65.

[34] Cf. Herbert Davis, introduction to The Complete Plays of William Congreve (Chicago, 1967), p. 8; Harold Love, Congreve (Oxford, 1974), pp. 45-7. Love (pp. 48-57) also relates 'the thinness of some of the individual portraits' to the point that, as in classical New Comedy, this is a play about the decay and survival of a family (and so, of a dynasty, and a hereditary oligarchy).

[35] The Times, 23 July 1969, p. 11.

Mellefont and Cynthia, are to marry the following day. The occasion is a celebratory dinner that provides the social framework for a double legal ceremony: Lord Touchwood is to sign the documents constituting his nephew Mellefont as his heir, and putting him in immediate 'possession of a fair estate' (V,i.76); he and Sir Paul are to sign the writings of settlement and jointure confirming Cynthia's financial status as Mellefont's wife. Brisk and Lord Froth are present not only as guests but as witnesses.

While 'the marriage of Mellefont and Cynthia' remains 'the main business of the play,' the major interest is transferred to the barrier-figures, Maskwell and Lady Touchwood, and to the 'gulling' actions by which they seek to prevent this marriage.[36] Maskwell, the lowborn dependent, is trying to substitute himself in Mellefont's place both as Lord Touchwood's heir and as Cynthia's husband. It is prodigiously difficult: he must dominate the characters concerned when the time arrives for the signing; and he must somehow gain possession of Cynthia, even though this means double-crossing his paranoid ally Lady Touchwood. And all must be done 'before the company break up' (III, 127-8).

He could have settled for the 'fair estate' and presumably got away with it, with audience applause; but whether through avarice, love, the rogue's delight in outrageous deceptions, or all three motives together, he tries to capture Cynthia and her dowry as well, and over-reaches himself. As a rogue-hero like Jonson's Volpone, he may cheat fools with impunity, but when his activities 'threaten the welfare of some good and innocent people, and finally all of society,' he must be stopped . . . and . . . punished.'[37] The representatives of the Touchwood and Plyant families, with the exception of Cynthia, are not impressive, either fools or 'honest, well-meaning' but not very perspicacious men. But on Cynthia's marriage with Mellefont depend the survival of not only two aristocratic families, but also, symbolically, their class and their society.

What is unusual is the extent to which Maskwell is depicted (admittedly mainly by the extravagantly-spoken Lady Touchwood) as a figure of outright evil: as 'a sedate, a thinking villain, whose black blood runs temperately bad,' or as a 'mollifying devil' (I,ii, 27-28, 71). Etherege's Dorimant had been accused and cursed in a similar fashion by Mrs Loveit, but with a less exclusively melodramatic effect.[38]

---

[36] Corman, p. 358.

[37] Corman, *ibid.*

[38] Cf. J. Douglas Canfield, 'Religious Language and Religious Meaning in Restoration Comedy,' *SEL*, XX (1980), 385-406, see p. 390.

Maskwell is defeated in Act V, yet has come very close to success, which is now redefined in terms of spiriting away Cynthia in a coach with Saygrace and himself for an immediate secret marriage. His defeat comes about apparently by chance: Cynthia's alertness in grasping the potential dangers of the changed rendezvous, and her flukily timely encounters with Careless and Mellefont, lead her to seize the chance to overhear the confrontation between Maskwell and Lady Touchwood. And by chance Lord Touchwood has come along, in a suitable frame of mind, to overhear it with her. The crucial confrontation has itself come about because Lady Touchwood has learnt, too soon, what Maskwell told her husband about his desire to marry Cynthia.

Aubrey Williams is in no doubt that all these chances are brought about through Divine Providence; though (unlike Sir Paul, who appeals to Providence so often) it is necessary to take advantage of the helps that it offers. His position relies on the omnipresence of such ideas about Providence in the sermons and devotional writings of the time, and an equating of providential and poetic justice.[39]

Williams' position on *The Double-Dealer* has been vigorously attacked by John Barnard and B. Eugene McCarthy. Barnard argues that 'Williams' account seems to me deeply misleading and at odds with the whole ethos of Congreve's world,' and that Congreve's known 'use of the term "poetic justice" . . . is purely affective.'[40] McCarthy argues that as well as religious imagery there are many other kinds in the play, and that Maskwell's defeat happens because

> It seems to be of the nature of the evil imagination that since it is uncontrolled it eventually destroys itself; it outwits itself because it operates outside of control. Those who [like Careless or Cynthia] wait with patient ears and eyes for the not entirely understandable . . . events to unwind will succeed. If one wishes to identify this force that exposes villainy as Providence, so be it, but the play itself does not so suggest . . .[41]

The argument has in wider terms been continued by Canfield, who argues that 'the religious language' in four major Restoration comedies that he examines 'is both casual and purposeful, ironic and literal. It is typically casual and ironic in the mouths of the characters but purposeful and ultimately literal in the pen of the author.'[42] The

---

[39] Williams, chapter 7.

[40] 'Passion, "Poetical Justice," and Dramatic Law in *The Double-Dealer* and *The Way of the World,*' in Morris, pp. 95-129, see p. 101.

[41] 'Providence in Congreve's *The Double-Dealer,*' *SEL*, XIX (1979), 407-19, see pp. 413-4.

[42] Canfield, p. 385.

dispute continues. Clearly some uses of religious terms in *The Double-Dealer*, as in Lady Touchwood's furious soliloquy, come very close to literal meaning:

> Oh! That I were fire indeed, that I might burn the vile traitor to a hell of torments,—but he's damnation-proof, a devil already, and fire is his element (V,ii. 27-30)).

A disjunctive private conflict emerges in Cynthia's challenge to Mellefont either to circumvent Lady Touchwood, or to prove that she is indeed assisted by the Devil. If he does neither, she says, she won't marry him. Like several other elements in the plot it is simply lost sight of; even for her (persuaded, offstage, by Maskwell to accept the elopement plan) 'a fundamental discrepancy' is revealed 'between words and action'. And she shares 'the good characters' inability to recognize, let along deal with, evil'.[43]

That it should nonetheless be Cynthia, the primary truewit in the play, who has the key role in the unmasking of Maskwell, exposes the absurdity of his assumption that having got her away from the house he could somehow deceive or compel her to marry him. It is questionable however whether this would be recognized in performance.

Mellefont has the caste-marks of a truewit and certainly talks as one, in his two fine little duets with Cynthia. Yet Congreve's defence of him, in his epistle, as not being proved to be a fool merely because he is cheated by a superlatively cunning opponent, does not dispose of the objection that he lets himself be cheated far too easily. His gushingly naive responses to Maskwell ('Oh see, I see my rising sun! Light breaks through clouds upon me, and I shall live in day,' etc.[44]) demonstrate increasingly an inability to grasp the meaning of what is being said and done. He is shown up damagingly by the greater perspicuity of Careless, Cynthia and even Lord Touchwood. There is a certain aptness in Lady Froth's remark in Act II that 'he is too much a mediocrity'; and Maskwell clearly includes him in the category of 'fair-faced fools,' embodiments of 'the hungry gudgeon Credulity.' He is then like Maskwell a hybrid, combining features of the truewit, the Jonsonian gull, and the comedy romantic lead (typically nearly till the end unsuccessful in his intrigues). In terms of the standards of good and evil, his moral impeccability may count for more than his lack of efficacy; but he is neither impressive nor very interesting and the play is left without a hero, or anyone to

[43] Anthony Gosse, 'Plot and Character in Congreve's *Double-Dealer,' MLQ,* XXIX (1962), 274-88, see pp. 280-1.

[44] II, 350-1; cf. Dacier on joy, above; Lee, *The Duke of Guise* (1682), IV,i. 119-21.

whom our sympathies can firmly attach. Even Cynthia is too cool and restrained, a latent rather than an active force.

Maskwell's true opponent is then not the individual, Mellefont, but the group; and his initial 'shallow device,' of having Lady Plyant persuaded that Mellefont is out to seduce her, has a greater success than he had any right to expect, because it splits the group up. Lady Plyant is impervious to protestations of innocence; and Careless is effectively neutralised for most of the rest of the play by his preoccupation with seducing her in earnest. Until he has won her over, even Cynthia can have only brief consultations with Mellefont. Hence this first device, though not causally connected with Maskwell's later schemes, does make them feasible. Nonetheless Maskwell's dupes are not finally fools, but people of a true though limited wit; and while he can deceive them individually, he cannot indefinitely prevent them from conferring with, or overhearing, each other, or prevent the group from re-uniting against him. That these things should happen in time to frustrate his designs is not inevitable, as I've already mentioned.

Consideration of Lady Touchwood raises in its most acute form the problem of mixed literary idioms. John Barnard has argued that in certain of the serious scenes there is a shift from a naturalistic to an 'affective' mode of dialogue, a heightened, artificial language of passion, as used in much Restoration tragedy. He sees this practice, ostensibly santioned by the Horatian epigraph, as a serious artistic blunder. Now unquestionably Lady Touchwood does at certain crises use such language, but what is uncertain is whether the playgoers of 1693 were instead expected to recognize that she is an instinctive playactor, a self-cast tragedy queen. At certain moments her words clearly reflect those of Roxana in Lee's *The Rival Queens*, though unlike Brisk and Sir Paul in relation to the same play she is not deliberately making direct quotations.[45] Still, the polarity between tragic and comic acting styles at this time was such that to make a character within a comedy adopt an heroic manner and diction would presumably have necessarily involved a calculated creation of a sense of burlesque.

Lady Touchwood can be at once taken seriously and ironically: her passions are intense enough, but her elevated rantings are undercut by the cool cynicism of Maskwell; and in the wider comic context the reflection of them in the gushings of Lady Plyant renders them absurd. Yet she remains a formidable stage-figure, even if, as Harold Love says, she 'is never permitted to resemble a credible human being.'[46]

[45] IV,vi. 33-5; cf. I,i.20-1; IV,ii. 63-5.
[46] *Congreve*, p. 45.

The fools, Brisk, the Froths and the Plyants, whose social inter-course and intrigues take up half the stage-time of the first four acts, exhibit a careful graduation from the almost-wit Brisk to the complete ninny Lord Froth. They are fine, not gross, fools, unlike the people at Lady Whiffler's, and exhibit doubtless what many took to be genuine wit, though it is reduced to mere verbal self-display, in which 'figures of speech enlarge the most trivial actions to epic proportions.'[47] Cynthia says, 'these have quality and education, wit and fine conversation, are received and admired by the world. . .'; yet their wit is false, their conversation pretentious and trivial. Congreve is redefining what it is to be a true wit, in the direction of verbal and moral restraint. Notwithstanding the Juvenalian exposure of their follies and failings, they are full of exuberant life.

Despite the relatively rudimentary nature of their intrigues, the triangles Sir Paul — Lady Plyant — Careless and Lord Froth — Lady Froth — Brisk parallel and contrast with the serious cuckolding triangle Lord Touchwood — Lady Touchwood — Maskwell. Where Lady Touchwood's immorality is destructively evil, Lady Froth and Lady Plyant are such butterflies that their promiscuity is merely funny, and such as their husbands richly deserve. A son for Sir Paul may be the best gift Providence can provide. A key (and historically authentic) factor in this society, that makes it so fragile, is its desperate lack of fecundity: there are single offspring only, or none at all. Few were born and fewer still survived. A relatively recent turn towards shows of fondness for children is satirised in Lady Froth's fussing over her Sappho.[48]

The main action is then serious in itself, yet our responses to it are ironically modified by the parallels in the subsidiary plot-strands. Like Lady Touchwood's ranting, Maskwell's villainous double-dealing is matched at the comic level by that of Careless and Brisk. The original casting of the serious actor Kynaston as Lord Touchwood indicates that he was not intended to be seen as, essentially, rendered ridiculous, like the two other cuckolded husbands.

This action is disconcerting in several ways. The opening sequence leads us to expect Mellefont to function as an active intriguer, but his unwillingness to dissimulate, as a means to controlling others, or to recognize Maskwell's dissimulation, renders his schemes almost wholly ineffectual, up to the point where he puts on the physical disguise of the parson's gown, and reverses its intended

[47] Norman N. Holland, *The First Modern Comedies: the Significance of Etherege, Wycherley and Congreve,* 2nd edn. (Bloomington, 1967), p. 152.
[48] Cf. Laurence Stone, *The Family, Sex and Marriage in England, 1500-1800,* abridged edn. (Harmondsworth, 1979), pp. 42, 56, 261, 272-84.

purpose. The meaning of the action is almost lost when Cynthia and Mellefont in IV,i set up an inner drama of private happiness or rejection independent of considerations of property or status. Maskwell's major plot is frustrated not primarily through a counter-intrigue but an *anagnorisis*, in V,iv. And when the villains are defeated in the bustling final scene they simply vanish, giving place to a brief, optimistic blessing on the lovers, and a dark warning about 'base treach'ry.' In the flawed, pragmatic world of Revolution England, Cynthia and Mellefont together represent the best hope there is for a more wisely governed society.

Much has been said by critics about the shortcomings of this play, by comparison with the masterpieces that followed. Maximilian Novak, who sees it as 'an exciting failure,' considers that Congreve tried to combine in it too many incompatible elements, creating 'three worlds: a verbal world of grotesque realism, one of high comedy and wit, and another of genuine evil suggested by chthonic imagery.' John Barnard argues that 'the structure is basically affective — moral, character and intrigue are not each inseparably part of the other.' Norman N. Holland believes that 'the play fails because Mellefont is so woefully inadequate as a hero,' though his 'natural goodness' points towards a real happiness beyond the reach either of folly or wisdom, akin to the ethos of eighteenth century sentimentalism. On the contrary side, Brian Corman argues that it does have 'form, unity and coherence,' even if finally it is 'not wholly satisfying.' And Anthony Gosse has characterised it as 'an ironic, dark comedy,' that achieves a unified complex effect.[49]

I take it to be a frequently dark yet genuine comedy, in which most of the characters are playacting, posturing or creating false appearances, and a few are trying to see truly. If it is a flawed play, its distinguished recent stage history demonstrates that it possesses a unique appeal, and considerable merits, as a lesser work of a great dramatic artist.

[49] Novak, *William Congreve* (New York, 1971), pp. 105-6; Barnard, in Morris, p. 103; Holland, pp. 157, 160; Corman, pp. 357, 365; Gosse, p. 278.

STAGE HISTORY

The date of the first performance is not known, but was probably in early November 1693, rather than in October where *The London Stage* places it (I, 428).[50] Publication was announced in *The London Gazette* of 4-7 December; and though the time lapse between the premiere and publication for *The Old Bachelor* had been no more than a week, about a month was evidently more normal for this decade.[51] Dryden writing on 12 December reported that by then the play had been acted eight times, which were probably not consecutive or he should have said so, but they need not have been far apart (*WCLD*, p. 95). Swift writing from Moor Park in Surrey on 6 December asked his brother to 'send me word immediately, how it succeeded, well, ill or indifferently . . .' He had evidently already heard from him about the date of the premiere ('if it were but acted when you say . . .'), but nothing more. His clear intention to send his complimentary verses to be printed with the play, if news came of its good success, indicates that he was taken by surprise by its being published as quickly as it was.[52]

The Gentleman's Journal of November 1693 comments: 'I need not say anything of Mr. *Congreve's Double-Dealer* (the only new Play since my last) after the Character which Mr. *Dryden* has given of it . . .' (p. 374). The monthly issues of this periodical tended to appear at some time during the month following their ostensible dates; and clearly this passage in the November issue was written with knowledge of the printed quarto, in which Dryden's 'Character' appeared, i.e. after 4 December. It would appear that the performances had begun too late in November to be mentioned in the October issue.

The audiences' reception of the play, as already noticed, bitterly upset the dramatist, but by comparison with the dismal failures of most other new plays of the surrounding seasons was 'indifferent' rather than 'ill.' John Downes in *Roscius Anglicanus* (1708) counted it as one of the three 'good Plays' of the time, with special mention of

---

[50] This section is indebted to Emmett L. Avery, *Congreve's Plays on the Eighteenth-Century Stage* (New York, 1951) and to *The London Stage*. Both provide cast-lists, and Avery has extensive comments on performers.

[51] Judith A. Milhous and R.D. Hume, 'Dating Play Premières from Publication Data, 1660-1700,' *Harvard Library Bulletin*, XXII (1974), 374-405, see p. 396.

[52] *The Correspondence of Jonathan Swift*, ed. H. Williams (Oxford, 1963), I, 14; cf. *The Poems of Jonathan Swift*, ed. H. Williams, 2nd edn. (Oxford, 1958), 43-50.

the 'Unparrell'd' performances in these of Doggett (Sir Paul Plyant) and Mrs Barry (Lady Touchwood) (p. 42).

The cast for the initial run was a fine one, very carefully related to the demands of the play, as has been indicated in the section on sources. A command performance was provided for Queen Mary, on 13 January 1694, in which Colley Cibber acquitted himself very well, at one day's notice, in Kynaston's role as Lord Touchwood.[53]

Records of performances before 1703 are very scanty, but Dryden's statement that this comedy, 'which was never very takeing,' was acted on 4 March 1699, may be matched with a comment in the advertisement for a performance at Lincoln's Inn Fields on 29 December 1703 that it was 'Never Acted there but Twice.' Two appearances in the March 1699 revival may well have been all there were from the time Betterton's company had opened in that theatre in 1695 (*The London Stage*, I,509; II,49).

Throughout the eighteenth century *The Double-Dealer* remained almost always less popular than Congreve's other plays, yet built up a very respectable record, continuing to be revived up to 1788, with 153 known London performances. From 18 October 1718, when it was revived, after 15 years, at John Rich's Lincoln's Inn Theatre, it retained a place in the repertory of at least one theatre company almost continuously through to 1759, missing only three seasons (1734-5, 1747-8 and 1753-4). Up to the 1733-4 season it remained the preserve of Rich's company, which had moved into the new Covent Garden Theatre in 1732. During this period it was not spectacularly popular, with a maximum of five showings in one season and more often two or three. In 1735-6 it appeared for the first time in the century at Drury Lane, being acted thirteen times, in addition to once at Covent Garden, the most in any season. This revival probably came about through the presence at Drury Lane of James Quin, who had till then held the role of Maskwell in the other company, and was now matched with first class colleagues, notably Benjamin Griffin as Sir Paul and Catherine Clive as Lady Froth, in whom, 'as in the rest of her comic characters,' Thomas Davies considered her 'superior to all actresses.'[54]

---

[53] *An Apology for the Life of Colley Cibber*, ed. B.R.S. Fone (Ann Arbor, 1968), p. 104.

[54] *Dramatic Miscellanies*, III, 324. Davies and Cross record that in the performance of 1 November 1756,

> when Brisk (Mr Woodward) was reading the Verses with Lady Froth (Mrs Clive) instead of observing, with the Author, that her Ladyship's Coachman, John, had a red Face, said *because Yr. Ladyship has a red face*, & because Mrs Clive is of that Complexion the Audience burst into a loud roar, to her no small Mortification; but she behav'd well & took no Notice of it.

(Cross, cited in *The London Stage*, IV, 562; Davies, ibid., differs slightly.)

The success at Drury Lane provoked a vigorous and lengthy attack on the play by Aaron Hill, in *The Prompter* of 11 November 1735. He regarded it, despite the merits of its plot-management and characterisation, as *'fundamentally bad,'* because its Fable. . .is *ill-chosen.* . . *A cold, deliberate, thinking Villain'* like Maskwell, who 'laughs at the very Notion of Virtue, is only to be corrected at TYBURN.' Lady Touchwood is equally *'deformed* and *diabolical,* . . . and the Lighter Characters [are] *obscene.'*

As the Drury Lane production began to wane in popularity, in 1738-9, the other company revived its own; and for the next twenty years the play appeared a few times in nearly every season in one theatre or the other, though most often at Covent Garden. During Garrick's management of Drury Lane (1747-76) he tried it only occasionally, with no participation by himself.

After 1759 it was revived eight times, for the most part briefly and with little success: in 1761-2 (Drury Lane, one performance), 1772-3 (Drury Lane, two), 1775-6 (Covent Garden, one; Haymarket, two), 1776-7 (Covent Garden, one), 1781-2 (Covent Garden, three), 1784-5 (Drury Lane, seven) and 1787-8 (Covent Garden, three). John Philip Kemble, who acted Maskwell on 4 April 1785, and three times in 1787-8, tried it out once, with a text cut by himself, on 27 February 1802. This drew a ferocious reaction from *The Monthly Mirror* (XIII, 27 February 1802), to the effect that:

> . . .Its wit does not atone for its indecency, and even its admirable plot, perfect as it is, . . .serves only to unfold scenes of grossness too shocking for exhibition on a moral stage. . . The whole mass is infectious, and defies any attempt at reform or qualification . . . Should . . . another representation be hazarded, we hope the public, which with difficulty suppressed its indignation on this evening, will testify the most decided reprobation of a play to which no female can listen without emotions of shame, and which must excite the utmost abhorrence in every virtuous mind.

It is not surprising that the play seems not to have been revived again till this century.

James Quin, a stocky man with a 'solemn declamatory Way' of speaking, dominated the role of Maskwell, either with Rich's company or at Drury Lane (1735-40), from 1718 to 28 January 1752. Davies mentions it as one of many in which he was 'most judicious and pleasing.'[55] Lacey Ryan kept the part of Careless with Rich's company continuously from 1718 to 1752, and played it once more in October 1758. Sir Paul Plyant was played in succession by Pack,

---

[55] *An Apology for the Life of Mr. T.C., Comedian* (1740), p. 138; Davies, *Memoirs of the Life of David Garrick, Esq.* (1780), I, 30.

Benjamin Griffin (LIF, 1720-21, Drury Lane, 1735-40), Phipps (1721-2), and then John Hippisley, who held the role in Rich's company for twenty five years. Charles Macklin took it on at Drury Lane in 1741-2, and again at Covent Garden in 1750-52 and 1776, it being remembered by Victor as one in which he was 'excellent.' Samuel Foote evoked mixed and on the whole unfavourable reactions ('he gave a loose to the most ridiculous burlesque, and the vilest grimace').[56]

The fine actresses who participated included, as Lady Plyant, Mrs Macklin and Peg Woffington (Davies recalled 'with pleasure her whimsical discovery of passion, and her awkwardly assumed prudery'—*Memoirs*, I, 308); as Lady Froth, Catherine Clive, Georgiana Bellamy and Miss Pope; and as Lady Touchwood, Mrs Pritchard and Mrs Taylor.

The reviewers of the 1787 revival gave their highest praise to Kemble as Maskwell: 'In execution, as well as in conception, his *Double Dealing* yields to no acting, past or present' (*The World*, 30 November). But despite the praise given to the performers, both *The World* and *The Public Advertiser* (1 December) deplored the absence of what the latter called 'a moral tendency.' The script, already trimmed to reduce its improprieties, or to reduce running time, had been specially re-cut by Thomas Sheridan for the 1775-7 revival, and was to be altered again by Kemble in 1802; but it was not possible to transform the nature of the action with its adulteries and allegations of incest into something positively exemplary. The removal from the script of profanities and over-explicitness about sex doubtless prolonged its theatrical life some 40 years, with a fairly severe loss of pungency.[57]

In the twentieth century the play was first revived by the Stage Society for two performances at the Queen's Theatre on 14 and 15 May 1916. Montague Summers, who assisted with the production, mentions in *The Restoration Theatre* (1934) that he was able to ensure that the full original script was used and also that certain of the Restoration stage conventions were retained, such as having the curtain raised throughout (p. 325).

The most noteworthy subsequent London productions include,

[56] Benjamin Victor, *The History of the Theatres of London and Dublin, from the Year 1730 to the Present Time* (Dublin, 1761), I, 100. Davies, *Memoirs*, etc., I, 191; cf. Avery, pp. 103-4.

[57] Cf. Avery, pp. 163-5. Acting editions include one of 1772, for Covent Garden (copy reported at Duke University); *Bell's British Theatre*, Vol. XIII (1777), for Drury Lane; Sheridan's in *The New English Theatre*, Vol. IX (1777), for Covent Garden; and Kemble's [1802], for Drury Lane.

first, the Old Vic's in September 1959, 'a hit at both the Edinburgh Festival and in London.' Anthony Gosse observes that 'For most of the reviewers, it was extraordinarily funny.'[58]

In July 1969 the English Stage Society mounted an economy-style production directed by William Gaskill at the Royal Court Theatre, full of vivacity and attack. Irving Wardle in *The Times* (23 July 1969) described it however as,

> over-careful and dislocated: and you take away a memory of sharply isolated moments rather than a purposeful flow of dramatic energy . . . The production is most alive when it is furthest from comedy: in Judy Parfitt's murderously frustrated Lady Touchwood and John Castle's Maskwell.

The National Theatre's production, which opened on 27 September 1978, in the Olivier Theatre in the new complex, directed by Peter Woods, was extremely competent and lavish, though to some tastes over-intellectual and insufficiently harsh. Robert Stephens' Maskwell was played very cool. He 'humanises the hanky-panky, performing it with a strangely doleful look, as if no one in the world were more overburdened or put-upon than he . . . At [times] his face becomes mottled and twisted with the sheer mental strain of stitching together all those plots and somehow making each consistent with each.' So said Benedict Nightingale in *The New Statesman* (6 October 1978), observing that 'this Maskwell is a delinquent Eeyore.' Irving Wardle in *The Times* (29 September) commented that Stephens gave 'this impenetrable Restoration Iago a human face.'

All the critics praised Michael Bryant's Sir Paul, in whom (said Nightingale) he found 'a skulking, shambling pathos.' Despite his wife's public insults and attacks, 'somehow the poor fellow convinces himself he's married a "fine, well-spoken woman," who treats him better than he deserves.' The conventional response to foolish uxoriousness is confuted 'with a man of feeling and humble dignity, who lets slip his embarrassment and misery in shy, apologetic monosyllables.'

The cast also included Sara Kestelman (Lady Touchwood), Dorothy Tutin (Lady Plyant), Brenda Blethyn (Lady Froth), Judi Bowker (Cynthia), Nicky Henson (Brisk), Nicholas Selby (Lord Froth), Dermot Crowley (Careless), John Harding (Mellefont) and Ralph Richardson (Lord Touchwood).

Tanya Moiseiwitsch's set on the open Olivier stage was described

[58] Gosse, op. cit., pp. 275-6. Reviews, e.g., *The Times*, 9 September 1959; *Punch*, 9 September; *Theatre World*, LV (October). Cf. Muir, in Morris, pp. 142-4.

by Irving Wardle as 'a magnificent timbered revolve, sprouting heraldic beasts, and honeycombed with exits, sliding panels, and handy casements for a quick getaway.' Its reverse side, Lady Touchwood's bedchamber, appeared briefly at the beginning with Maskwell 'heroically fulfilling the night's assignment.'[59]

The effect of the play in the theatre has evidently varied greatly, depending primarily on whether Maskwell was interpreted as a 'deformed and diabolical' villain, a 'poisonous . . . creature from another world,' in the manner of Quin (as we may deduce), and of John Castle, or instead as a rogue, in the manner of Robert Stephens, unscrupulous enough yet remaining within the comic order.

[59] Cf. reviews, *Observer*, 1 October 1978; *Listener*, 5 October; *Plays and Players*, December.

NOTE ON THE TEXT

THREE TEXTS have significant authority: those in the first and second quartos, of 1694 and 1706, and in *The Works of Mr. William Congreve* of 1710. A fourth, in the true second edition of *The Works* (called 'The THIRD') of 1719-20, contains some interesting substantive variants, but the revisions requested by him were probably in format only.[60]

It seems evident that Congreve took considerable care to secure clean texts, and in making revisions scrutinised every detail. Q1 contains a mere handful of surviving misprints, and of minor press-corrections, the one major aberration being the introduction, probably in the majority of copies, of a cancel leaf to replace the original G1, in which three words had been omitted.[61] Q2 is described on its titlepage as 'Revised,' the most significant changes being the deletion of the most outspoken passages in the dedicatory epistle, and of the more profane expressions in the dialogue. The 1710 *Works* is recommended in the author's preface 'as the least faulty Impression, which has yet been Printed; in which, Care has been taken both to Revise the Press, and to Review and Correct many Passages in the Writing.' For this play, the processes have been carried further of deleting or toning down 'profaneness and immorality,' and of literary improvement. In addition the acts have been divided into neoclassical 'French scenes,' with a new scene beginning whenever a character enters or leaves the stage. The cumulative effect is to establish a distinctly different version of the play, within the context of an edition that was designed to provide a refined literary experience to the gentleman-readers of the new age, rather than recollections of performances for the playgoers of the old.

The choice of an editorial policy that will serve this play, in Professor McKenzie's words, 'at its fullest and best' is not simple. Merely to reprint the Q1 version unrevised will not fulfil this purpose; and the revisions vary so much in their nature that it will not do, either, to treat all of them alike.

The treatment of scene-format is particularly problematic. In Q1 and Q2 the text is divided only by its separation into five acts: even the episode in the last part of Act IV, in Lady Touchwood's bed-

---

[60] The issues are more extensively discussed in McKenzie, pp. 37-54, in his article, 'When Congreve Made a Scene,' *Transactions of the Cambridge Bibliographical Society*, VII, pt. 3 (1979), 338-42, and in Holland, pp. 125-37.

[61] See Longer Notes, No. 2.

chamber, is not distinguished as a separate scene. Analysis of entrances and exits reveals that great variety has been introduced in the ways exits are related to adjacent entries, with longer or shorter passages of dialogue intervening, and also, in the number of characters involved. This serves to counteract the danger of visual monotony, incurred through having a single set present virtually throughout. In five instances (three of them in Act V) exits are staggered, to avoid creating scissors-effects, as characters depart in opposite directions. On fifteen occasions (eight in Act V) a character remains alone on stage at the end of a sequence long enough to speak in soliloquy before another character enters to him.

This theatrical subtlety is almost completely sacrificed in W1, with the introduction of 'French scenes.' In an increasingly rapid-moving comedy of intrigue, W1's format works, in a fashion, for the first three and a half acts, through the elimination of the intervals between exits and entries. It becomes very awkward, when the remainder of Act IV breaks into 14 scenes, and Act V into no less than 24. Two more such scene-breaks at the end of Act V have been avoided only by delaying the exit of Lady Touchwood, and having Maskwell not removed from the stage at all, in each case in clear defiance of the sense of the text. Otherwise the reader's attention would have been distracted even more than it already is by the intrusion of scene-numbers and long lists of characters present.

Professor McKenzie has argued very cogently that by the time he was writing *Love for Love* in 1694-5 Congreve had the neoclassical, 'and no other, scene structure in mind,' and shaped his play accordingly (p. 51). I do not agree that this is consistently valid in relation to Congreve's practice in *The Double-Dealer*. Some 'scenes' were clearly created as coherent units (e.g. the last in Act I and the first in Act IV), but elsewhere the true units are larger sections within the acts, and the acts themselves. As Dr. Peter Holland has said, 'one effect' of the imposition of the scene-structure in W1 is 'to make of each scene a unit with a separable weight of meaning, rather than to accept the fluidity and over-arching structure of the act as a whole.' Moreover, six of the 'scenes' so created are 'ridiculously short,' amounting to a single speech of five lines or less, three such scenes being generated by 'the pattern of hiding' in the Act IV bedchamber episode (Holland, pp. 135-6).

In my view the play may be presented 'at its fullest and best' by relating it, primarily, to its historical moment, 1693, and to dramatic realization at that time. And secondly, one includes in the text such later literary improvements as genuinely enhance the style yet do not detract from the racy vigour and toughness of the play of 1693.

For these purposes, the neoclassical scene format which divorces it from the theatre will not do. The format of the quartos, in which the acts are wholly undivided, has authority, but does nothing to reveal the dramatic structures within the acts. The introduction of scene-divisions whenever the stage is momentarily empty is manifestly unauthoritative and to a degree arbitrary, yet it does serve to expose the larger dramatic movements, and the more intricate structures of Acts IV and V (this is quite distinct from the practice of A.C. Ewald in the original Mermaid, who introduced quite unjustified changes of place between '*The Gallery*' and '*An Apartment*' or '*A Room*', and unnecessary exits and entrances). The muted scene-divisions that I have introduced are to be regarded as an editorial modification to the format of Q1, as an aid to the reader.

Congreve's removal or toning down of the sexual and profane elements in his dialogue were evidently motivated partly by a desire to bring the text into compliance with the criteria of propriety being imposed on the script in the theatre, by the threat of prosecution, and partly to comply with society's and his own altered standards of gentility. The effect was unfortunate: the losses include 'the whole point of' the Plyants' 'castrated relationship,' and also much of the verbal evidence that Lady Touchwood 'and her accomplice are devils,' which makes Mellefont's failure against her excusable (Holland, pp. 127-9). Clearly the ruder and more blasphemous readings of Q1 must be retained.

The question of how to treat the stylistic revisions of Q2 and W1 is less straightforward. On the one hand, Congreve first wrote the play when he was only twenty-three, and achieved a prodigiously finer artistry in his later plays: his own mature judgements deserve respect. On the other hand, some of the shifts towards a smoother, more felicitous style involve a significant loss of the racy, colloquial force of the original readings, and several cause a distinct weakening of the sense (e.g. V,iii. 34: that thou'rt / thou art). Other revisions correct grammatical faults, increase the lucidity or precision of ideas, reduce verbosity, expand abbreviated forms, or in some cases abbreviate ('you are' becomes 'you're') with a marked tautening of speech-rhythm. Furthermore, Congreve was experimenting with transcribing natural speech-modes, with broken sentences or phrases, and pauses of differing length rendered by the combination of a dash with a comma, semi-colon, colon or full stop; and some refinements to this technique were made in Q2 and W1.

In view of the differing nature of these revisions, it is necessary to examine all such choices between readings on their individual merits. I have based my text on Q1, and all choices in favour of Q1 readings are covered by the general justification of preserving the essential qualities of the Q1 text. Such readings from Q2 and W1 as are introduced into the text are noticed in the annotations, with a brief indication of the main reason for choosing the Q2 or W1 variant.

In general, the policy of this series has been followed in modernising spellings (standardizing 'I'gad' to 'egad', 'Gad's bud' to 'Gadsbud', etc.), but conserving the original punctuation, though it has been in some places lightened, or modified where it was radically incompatible with modern usage. The standard New Mermaid format has been introduced in the treatment of speech-prefixes, stage-directions, and the use of italic in the *Dramatis Personae*.

FURTHER READING

Lawrence Bartlett, *William Congreve: a Reference Guide* (Boston, Mass., 1979).

Anthony Gosse, 'Plot and Character in Congreve's *Double-Dealer,*' *MLQ*, XXIX (1962), 274-88.

Harriet Hawkins, *Likenesses of Truth in Elizabethan and Restoration Drama* (Oxford, 1972).

Norman N. Holland, *The First Modern Comedies: the Significance of Etherege, Wycherley and Congreve* (Cambridge, Mass., 1959).

Robert D. Hume, *The Development of English Drama in the Late Seventeenth Century* (Oxford, 1976).

John Loftis, Richard Southern, Marion Jones and A.H. Scouten, *Revels History of English Drama,* Vol. V, *1660-1750* (London, 1976).

Harold Love, *Congreve* (Oxford, 1974).

Brian Morris, ed., *Mermaid Critical Commentaries: William Congreve* (London, 1970) (NB. article by John Barnard).

Maximilian Novak, *William Congreve* (New York, 1971).

W.H. Van Voris, *The Cultivated Stance: the Design of Congreve's Plays* (Dublin, 1965).

Aubrey Williams, *An Approach to Congreve* (New Haven, Connecticut and London, 1979).

THE
Double-Dealer,
A
COMEDY.

Acted at the
THEATRE ROYAL,
By Their Majesties Servants.

Written by Mr. *CONGREVE*.

Interdum tamen, & vocem Comædia tollit.
Hor. Ar. Po.

LONDON,
Printed for *Jacob Tonson*, at the *Judges-Head* near
the *Inner-Temple-Gate* in *Fleet-street*. 1694.

Hor. Ar. Po. Q1 (Hor. Ar. Po./*Huic equidem consilio palman do: hic me magnifice effero, qui vim tantam in me & potestatum habeam tantae astutiae, vera dicendo ut eos ambos fallam.* Syr. in Terent. Heaut. Q2)

Interdum. . .*Po*. 'Yet even comedy at times raises its voice,' Horace, *Ars Poetica*, 1.93. See Introduction, pp. xix-xx.

Huic. . .*Heaut*. 'Oh I reckon this a Masterpiece of my Cunning: In this plot I triumph in having that mighty knack and faculty at Juggling as to cheat both of them, by telling the truth,' Syrus in Terence's *Heautontimorumenos*, ll. 709—11, translation from L. Echard *et al.*, *Terence's Comedies Made English* (1694), p. 135. See Introduction, pp. xv-xvi.

To the Right Honourable
CHARLES MONTAGU,
one of the
Lords of the *TREASURY*

SIR,

I heartily wish this play were as perfect as I intended it, that it might be more worthy your acceptance; and that my dedication of it to you might be more becoming that honour and esteem which I, with everybody who is so fortunate as to know you, have for you. It had your countenance when yet unknown; and now it is made public, it wants your protection.

And give me leave, without any flattery to you or vanity in myself, to tell my illiterate critics, as an answer to their impotent objections, that they have found fault with that which has been pleasing to you. This play in relation to my concern for its reputation succeeded before it was acted, for through your early patronage it had an audience of several persons of the first rank both in wit and quality; and their allowance of it was a consequence of your approbation. Therefore if I really wish it might have had a more popular

5

10

15

5 *is* W1 (are Q1)
6 *countenance* patronage
7 *it wants* Q1 (wants W2)
8-25 *And. . .expense* Q1 (*om.* Q2)
15 *allowance* approbation

DEDICATORY EPISTLE. This text preserves the particularly 'defying or hectoring' passages that were deleted in Q2, or revised to give a less subjective slant, and appeal more to the reader's own critical sense. The writer who so characterised Congreve's manner commented that Dryden had 'deluded him into a foolish imitation of his own way of angry prefaces' (*The London Stage*, I, 428); cf. preface, *Don Sebastian* (1690).

0.2 *Charles Montagu*. (1661-1715). A brilliant, aristocratic Whig politician, whose genius for public finance quickly led to his appointments as a commissioner, then a Lord of the Treasury (March 1692), its First Lord (1697), and also Chancellor of the Exchequer (1694). His elevation in 1692, when most high offices were held by Tories, 'gave great satisfaction to the Whigs, in whose esteem' he now stood 'second to Somers alone' (Macaulay, V, 2140). He fell from power in 1699, and became Baron Halifax in 1700, Earl of Halifax in 1714.

5 *is*. W1's 'is' gives a clear sense to 'everybody' (all those who 'are so fortunate as to know you') which becomes unambiguously the subject, with a correctly singular verb.

reception, it is not at all in consideration of myself, but because
I wish well, and would gladly contribute to the benefit of the
stage, and diversion of the town. They were (not long since) so
kind to a very imperfect comedy of mine, that I thought myself   20
justly indebted to them all my endeavours for an
entertainment that might merit some little of that applause,
which they were so lavish of, when I thought I had no title to
it. But I find they are to be treated cheaply, and I have been at
an unnecessary expense.   25

I would not have anybody imagine that I think this play
without its faults, for I am conscious of several, and ready to
own 'em; but it shall be to those who are able to find 'em out. I
confess I designed (whatever vanity or ambition occasioned
that design) to have written a true and regular comedy, but I   30
found it an undertaking which put me in mind of—*Sudet
multum, frustraque laboret ausus idem.* And now to make
amends for the vanity of such a design, I do confess both the
attempt and the imperfect performance. Yet I must take the
boldness to say, I have not miscarried in the whole; for the   35
mechanical part of it is perfect. That I may say with as little
vanity, as a builder may say he has built a house according to
the model laid down before him, or a gardener that he has set
his flowers in a knot of such or such a figure. I designed the
moral first, and to that moral I invented the fable, and do not   40
know that I have borrowed one hint of it anywhere. I made the
plot as strong as I could, because it was single, and I made it
single, because I would avoid confusion, and was resolved to

---

24 *treated* entertained
27-8 *and. . .out* Q1 (*om.* Q2)
36 *perfect* Q1 (regular W1)

---

20 *a very imperfect comedy.* I.e., *The Old Bachelor;* cf. Introduction, pp. x-xi;
    Summers, IV, 182.
30 *true and regular.* Complying with generic prescriptions, and observing the
    unities.
31-2 *Sudet. . .idem.* One 'may sweat much and yet toil in vain while attempting the
    same.' The context is relevant: 'My aim shall be poetry, so moulded from the
    familar that anybody may hope for the same success, may sweat. . .same: such is
    the power of order and connexion, such the beauty, that may crown the
    commonplace' (Horace, *Ars Poetica,* ll. 240-3 [Loeb]).
39-40 *I designed. . .fable.* This complies with René le Bossu's 'first rule' for 'the
    writer of an heroic poem,' obligatory because the epic was held to function as an
    instructive moral allegory. Dryden had extended the rule 'for the same reason to
    all dramatic poetry' ('The Grounds of Criticism in Tragedy,' Watson, I, 248).

preserve the three unities of the drama, which I have visibly
done to the utmost severity. This is what I ought not to   45
observe upon myself; but the ignorance and malice of the
greater part of the audience is such, that they would make a
man turn herald to his own play, and blazon every character.
However, sir, this discourse is very impertinent to you, whose
judgement much better can discern the faults than I can excuse   50
them, and whose good nature, like that of a lover, will find out
those hidden beauties (if there are any such) which it would be
great immodesty in me to discover. I think I don't speak
improperly when I call you a *lover* of poetry, for it is very well
known she has been a very kind mistress to you; she has not   55
denied you the last favour, and she has been fruitful to you in a
most beautiful issue.—If I break off abruptly here, I hope
everybody will understand that it is to avoid a commendation,
which, as it is your due, would be most easy for me to pay, and
too troublesome for you to receive.   60

I have since the acting of this play hearkened after the
objections which have been made to it, for I was conscious
where a true critic might have put me upon my defence. I was
prepared for the attack; and am pretty confident I could have

44-9 *which. . .However* Q1 (*om.* W1)
49 *impertinent* inappropriate
53 *in* Q1 (for Q2)
55 *very kind* Q2 (kind Q1)
56 *and she* W1 (you have enjoyed her and she Q1)
56 *to you* W1 (*not in* Q1)
64 *the* W1 (their Q1)

---

44 *the three unities.* Despite his critical advocacy for 'the observation of the three
unities, time, place and action' as 'the mechanic beauties of the plot,'Dryden
typified his own practice, and that of his age, in acknowledging that in *Don
Sebastian* he had 'followed them only at a distance; for the genius of the English
cannot bear too regular a play; we are given to a variety, even to a debauchery of
pleasure' (Watson, I, 247; II, 49). Hence Congreve is defying accepted wisdom.
45 *the utmost severity.* They are preserved with a remarkable, but not 'the *utmost*
severity': see Introduction, pp. xx-xxi.
53-7 *I think. . .issue.* Montagu's limited literary output was remarkable less for its
quality than for the rewards it had earned him. His elegy for the death of
Charles II had gained him the patronage of the Earl of Dorset; and *The Hind and
the Panther Transversed: to the Story of the Country-Mouse and the City-Mouse*
(anti-Catholic satire, written in collaboration with Matthew Prior) brought him,
in 1689, a pension of £500 a year, and a seat in the Convention Parliament.
55-6 *very. . .you.* W1's readings eliminate repetition of the sexual metaphor, with
compensating changes to restore the emphaticness of the praise.
64 *the.* W1's 'the' avoids the awkward use of a plural pronoun, 'their', to relate to a
singular 'true critic.'

vindicated some parts, and excused others; and where there 65
were any plain miscarriages, I would most ingenuously have
confessed 'em. But I have not heard anything said sufficient to
provoke an answer. Some little snarling and barking there has
been, but I don't know one well-mouthed cur that has opened
at all. That which looks most like an objection, does not relate 70
in particular to this play, but to all or most that ever have been
written, and that is soliloquy. Therefore I will answer it, not
only for my own sake, but to save others the trouble, to whom
it may hereafter be objected.

I grant, that for a man to talk to himself appears absurd and 75
unnatural; and indeed it is so in most cases; but the
circumstances which may attend the occasion make great
alteration. It oftentimes happens to a man to have designs
which require him to himself, and in their nature cannot admit
of a confidant. Such, for certain, is all villainy; and other less 80
mischievous intentions may be very improper to be
communicated to a second person. In such a case therefore the
audience must observe whether the person upon the stage
takes any notice of them at all or no. For if he supposes anyone
to be by, when he talks to himself, it is monstrous and 85
ridiculous to the last degree. Nay, not only in this case, but in
any part of a play, if there is expressed any knowledge of an
audience, it is insufferable. But otherwise, when a man in
soliloquy reasons with himself, and *pro*'s and *con*'s, and weighs
all his designs: we ought not to imagine that this man either 90
talks to us or to himself; he is only thinking, and thinking such
matter as were inexcusable folly in him to speak. But because
we are concealed spectators of the plot in agitation, and the
poet finds it necessary to let us know the whole mystery of his
contrivance, he is willing to inform us of this person's 95
thoughts; and to that end is forced to make use of the expedient
of speech, no other better way being yet invented for the
communication of thought.

Another very wrong objection has been made by some who
have not taken leisure to distinguish the characters. The hero 100
of the play, as they are pleased to call him (meaning
Mellefont), is a gull, and made a fool, and cheated. Is every

68-70 *Some. . .all* Q1 (*om.* Q2)
69 *opened* given tongue (of hounds)

75-98 *I grant. . .thought.* This discussion of soliloquy derives closely from that in
Francois Hédelin, Abbé d'Aubignac, *The Whole Art of the Stage,* etc. (1684),
III:8, p. 58.

man a gull and a fool that is deceived? At that rate I'm afraid
the two classes of men will be reduced to one, and the knaves
themselves be at a loss to justify their title: but if an open- 105
hearted, honest man, who has an entire confidence in one
whom he takes to be his friend, and whom he has obliged to be
so; and who (to confirm him in his opinion) in all appearance
and upon several trials has been so: if this man be deceived by
the treachery of the other; must he of necessity commence fool 110
immediately, only because the other has proved a villain? Ay,
but there was caution given to Mellefont in the first act by his
friend Careless. Of what nature was that caution? Only to give
the audience some light into the character of Maskwell, before
his appearance; and not to convince Mellefont of his treachery; 115
for that was more than Careless was then able to do: he never
knew Maskwell guilty of any villainy; he was only a sort of
man which he did not like. As for his suspecting his familiarity
with my Lady Touchwood: let 'em examine the answer that
Mellefont makes him, and compare it with the conduct of 120
Maskwell's character through the play.

I would have 'em again look into the character of Maskwell
before they accuse Mellefont of weakness for being deceived
by him. For upon summing up the enquiry into this objection,
[I] find they have only mistaken cunning in one character, for 125
folly in another.

But there is one thing, at which I am more concerned than
all the false criticisms that are made upon me, and that is, some
of the ladies are offended. I am heartily sorry for it, for I
declare I would rather disoblige all the critics in the world than 130
one of the fair sex. They are concerned that I have represented
some women vicious and affected. How can I help it? It is the
business of a comic poet to paint the vices and follies of
humankind; and there are but two sexes, that I know, *viz.*, men
and women, which have a title to humanity: and if I leave one 135
half of them out, the work will be imperfect. I should be very
glad of an opportunity to make my compliment to those ladies

122 *have 'em again* Q1 (beg 'em again to Q2)
123 *Mellefont* Q2 (anybody Q1)
125 *[I] find they have only* Ed. (find they have only Q1; it may be found they have
    Q2)
134 *that I know, viz.* Q1 (male and female Q2)

132-4 *It is. . .humankind.* This was orthodox doctrine, but audiences were proving
    increasingly intolerant of satire that touched themselves; cf. Thomas Durfey,
    The Marriage-Hater Match'd (1692), sig. A2ᵛ.

who are offended: but they can no more expect it in a comedy,
than to be tickled by a surgeon when he's letting 'em blood.
They who are virtuous or discreet I'm sure cannot be offended,   140
for such characters as these distinguish *them*, and make their
beauties more shining and observed: and they who are of the
other kind may nevertheless pass for such, by seeming not to
be displeased, or touched with the satire of this comedy. Thus
have they also wrongfully accused me of doing them a   145
prejudice, when I have in reality done them a service.

I have heard some whispering, as if they intended to accuse
this play of smuttiness and bawdy: but I declare I took a
particular care to avoid it, and if they find any in it, it is of
their own making, for I did not design it to be so understood.   150
But to avoid my saying anything upon a subject which has
been so admirably handled before, and for their better
instruction, I earnestly recommend to their perusal the epistle
dedicatory before the *Plain-Dealer*.

You will pardon me, sir, for the freedom I take of making   155
answers to other people, in an epistle which ought wholly to be
sacred to you: but since I intend the play to be so too, I hope I
may take the more liberty of justifying it, where it is in the
right. I hear a great many of the fools are angry at me, and I am
glad of it; for I writ at them, not to 'em. This is a bold   160
confession, and yet I don't think I shall disoblige one person
by it; for nobody can take it to himself without owning the
character.

I must now, sir, declare to the world, how kind you have
been to my endeavours; for in regard of what was well meant,   165
you have excused what was ill performed. I beg you would
continue the same method in your acceptance of this
dedication. I know no other way of making a return to that

---

140 *I'm sure cannot* Q1 (can hardly Q2; should not W1)
147-54 *I. . .Plain-Dealer* Q1 (*om.* W1)
147 *some. . .intended* Q1 (there are some who intend Q2)
148 *declare* Q1 (can hardly believe it, because Q2)
159-63 *I hear. . .character* Q1 (*om.* Q2)

140-4 *They. . .comedy.* 'But why. . .shou'd any at all of the truly vertuous be concern'd
[at the satire], *if those who are not so are distinguish'd from 'em?. . .*'(William
Wycherley, *The Plain-Dealer* [1676], dedicatory epistle, ll. 75-7).
147-50 *I have. . .understood.* Cf. Wycherley's complaint about '*those who ravish a
Poet's innocent words, and make 'em guilty of their own naughtiness*' (*idem*, ll.
28-9).

humanity you showed, in protecting an infant, but by enrolling it in your service, now that it is of age and come into 170 the world. Therefore be pleased to accept of this as an acknowledgement of the favour you have shown me, and an earnest of the real service and gratitude of,

SIR,

Your Most Obliged
Humble Servant
WILLIAM CONGREVE.

169 *humanity* Q2 (charity Q1)

---

169 *humanity.* Q2's reading is here more broadly complimentary, both to the dedicatee and the dedicator.

To my Dear Friend
Mr. Congreve,
On His COMEDY, called,
The Double-Dealer

Well then, the promised hour is come at last;
The present age of wit obscures the past:
Strong were our sires, and as they fought they writ,
Conqu'ring with force of arms and dint of wit;
Theirs was the giant race before the flood;   5
And thus, when Charles returned, our empire stood.
Like Janus he the stubborn soil manured,
With rules of husbandry the rankness cured:
Tamed us to manners, when the stage was rude;
And boisterous English wit with art endued.   10
Our age was cultivated thus at length;
But what we gained in skill we lost in strength.
Our builders were with want of genius curst;
The second temple was not like the first:
Till you, the best Vitruvius, come at length,   15
Our beauties equal, but excel our strength.
Firm Doric pillars found your solid base,
The fair Corinthian crowns the higher space;
Thus all below is strength, and all above is grace.
In easy dialogue is Fletcher's praise: 20

To. . .Congreve. Extensive headnotes and annotations are provided in Dryden,
Poems, IV, 2025-6, and *Works,* IV, 742-6. And cf. Thomas Fujimura, 'The
Personal Element in Dryden's Poetry,' *PMLA,* LXXXIX (1974), 1007-23.

5 *the giant race,* etc. See Genesis, 6:4.

7 *Janus.* Normally a Roman god of beginnings, some legends portrayed him as an
early king of Latium, who taught the Italians agriculture and other arts of
civilization; cf. Dryden's Note No. 6 to the First Satire of Persius (*Works,* IV,
278).

14 *The second temple.* The glory of the Temple at Jerusalem, as rebuilt after the
exile, was said to be, initially, 'as nothing' by comparison with Solomon's
(Haggai, 2:3).

15 *Vitruvius.* Author of the only book on architecture by an architect of Classical
Roman times to have survived.

20-1 *easy dialogue.* Dryden considered that Fletcher excelled in the dialogue of
gentlemen, and particularly in 'Repartee. . .a chase of wit kept up on both sides,
and skilfully managed' (*Works,* XVII, 48-9).

He moved the mind, but had not power to raise.
Great Jonson did by strength of judgement please;
Yet doubling Fletcher's force, he wants his ease.
In diff'ring talents both adorned their age;
One for the study, t'other for the stage.   25
But both to Congreve justly shall submit,
One matched in judgement, both o'er-matched in wit.
In him all beauties of this age we see:
Etherege his courtship, Southerne's purity,
The satire, wit, and strength of manly Wycherley.   30
All this in blooming youth you have achieved;
Nor are your foiled contemporaries grieved;
So much the sweetness of your manners move,
We cannot envy you because we love.
Fabius might joy in Scipio, when he saw   35
A beardless consul made against the law,
And join his suffrage to the votes of Rome;
Though he with Hannibal was overcome.
Thus old Romano bowed to Raphael's fame,
And scholar to the youth he taught became.   40

Oh that your brows my laurel had sustained,
Well had I been deposed if you had reigned!
The father had descended for the son;
For only you are lineal to the throne.

---

21 *not* Q1 (no Q2)
29 *courtship* courtliness
32 *Nor* Q2 (Now Q1)

---

30 *manly*. Allusion to Manly, hero of *The Plain-Dealer*.
32 *Nor*. Q1's 'Now' is clearly a misprint, producing a sense opposite to that intended.
35-8 'Had Scipio been as loveable as you, the envious Fabius would have rejoiced in his early fame and supported him, even though Fabius had in his own day been unsuccessful against Hannibal' (Kinsley). P. Cornelius Scipio Africanus (Major) first became consul in 205 B.C., aged 30 or 31. Custom required that a consul be a mature man (i.e., at least 40, though there was at that time no legal minimum age) and have held other senior public offices (Scipio had had only an aedileship, and military command in Spain). The conservative Fabius would have considered this elevation illegal, and did oppose his plan to attack Carthage.
39-40 An error: Raphael's master was Perugino, with whom for a time he collaborated as a pupil. Giulio Romano, nine years younger than Raphael, became the latter's pupil and chief assistant.

Thus when the state one Edward did depose,   45
A greater Edward in his room arose.
But now, not I, but poetry is cursed;
For Tom the second reigns like Tom the first.
But let 'em not mistake my patron's part;
Nor call his charity their own desert.   50
Yet this I prophesy: thou shalt be seen
(Though with some short parenthesis between)
High on the throne of wit; and seated there,
Not mine (that's little) but thy laurel wear.
Thy first attempt an early promise made;   55
That early promise this has more than paid.
So bold, yet so judiciously you dare,
That your least praise is to be regular.
Time, place, and action may with pains be wrought,
But genius must be born, and never can be taught.   60
This is your portion, this your native store;
Heaven that but once was prodigal before,
To Shakespeare gave as much; she could not give him more.

Maintain your post: that's all the fame you need;
For 'tis impossible you should proceed.   65
Already I am worn with cares and age;
And just abandoning th' ungrateful stage:
Unprofitably kept at Heaven's expense,
I live a rent-charge on his Providence:
But you, whom every Muse and Grace adorn,   70
Whom I foresee to better fortune born,
Be kind to my remains; and oh defend,
Against your judgement, your departed friend!
Let not the insulting foe my fame pursue,

74 *the* Q1 (th' Q2)

45-6 Edward II, deposed in 1327, was followed by his rightful successor, Edward
    III (as, by implication, Dryden, and James II, should have been).

47-8 The posts of poet laureate and historiographer royal, held by Dryden prior to
    the Revolution of 1688, were then given to Thomas Shadwell. After his death in
    November 1692, Thomas Rymer became Historiographer and Nahum Tate
    Poet Laureate.

49-50 The Earl of Dorset, responsible as Lord Chamberlain for appointing
    Shadwell, Rymer and Tate, nonetheless remained a generous patron to Dryden,
    and was under no illusions about the respective literary merits of Dryden and
    his rivals.

60 Proverbial, *'Poeta nascitur non fit,'* Tilley P451.

67 *just. . .stage.* 'A reference to *Love Triumphant,* which was produced in 1694 and
    which Dryden considered his farewell to the stage' (*Works,* IV, 746).

But shade those laurels which descend to you: 75
And take for tribute what these lines express:
You merit more; nor could my love do less.

John Dryden.

PROLOGUE
Spoken by Mrs. Bracegirdle

Moors have this way (as story tells) to know
Whether their brats are truly got, or no:
Into the sea the new-born babe is thrown,
There, as instinct directs, to swim or drown;
A barbarous device, to try if spouse   5
Have kept religiously her nuptial vows!

  Such are the trials poets make of plays:
Only they trust to more inconstant seas;
So does our author this his child commit
To the tempestuous mercy of the pit,   10
To know if it be truly born of wit.

  Critics avaunt; for you are fish of prey,
And feed like sharks upon an infant play.
Be every monster of the deep away;
Let's have a fair trial, and a clear sea.   15

  Let nature work, and do not damn too soon,
For life will struggle long, ere it sink down:
And will at least rise thrice, before it drown.
Let us consider, had it been our fate,
Thus hardly to be proved legitimate!   20
I will not say, we'd all in danger been,
Were each to suffer for his mother's sin;
But by my troth I cannot avoid thinking
How nearly some good men might have 'scaped sinking.
But Heaven be praised, this custom is confined   25
Alone to the offspring of the Muses' kind:
Our Christian cuckolds are more bent to pity;
I know not one Moor-husband in the city.
I' th' good man's arms the chopping bastard thrives,

5 *barbarous* punning on Barbary   6 *Have* Q1 (Has W1)
18 *And will* W1 (Let it Q1)
26 *the* Q1 (th' Q2)
29 *chopping* big and vigorous

---

1 *as story tells.* The story remains unidentified.
18 *And. . .drown.* 'Correspondingly this play, even if it proves misbegotten, should
   at least be allowed to reach its third performance' (the author's benefit). Q1's
   'Let it' is unnecessarily repetitive, and confuses the analogy.

For he thinks all his own that is his wife's.   30

    Whatever fate is for this play designed,
The poet's sure he shall some comfort find:
For if his Muse has played him false, the worst
That can befall him is to be divorced;
You husbands judge, if that, be to be cursed.   35

DRAMATIS PERSONAE

Men

MASKWELL, *a villain; pretended friend to Mellefont,*   Mr. Betterton
gallant to Lady Touchwood, and in love with
Cynthia
LORD TOUCHWOOD, *uncle to Mellefont*   Mr. Kynaston
MELLEFONT, *promised to, and in love with Cynthia*   Mr. Williams
CARELESS, *his friend*   Mr. Verbruggen
LORD FROTH, *a solemn coxcomb*   Mr. Bowman
BRISK, *a pert coxcomb*   Mr. Powell
SIR PAUL PLYANT, *an uxorious, foolish, old knight;*   Mr. Doggett
brother to Lady Touchwood, and father to
Cynthia

Women

LADY TOUCHWOOD, *in love with Mellefont*   Mrs. Barry
CYNTHIA, *daughter to Sir Paul by a former wife,*   Mrs. Bracegirdle
promised to Mellefont
LADY FROTH, *a great coquette; pretender to poetry,*   Mrs. Mountfort
wit, and learning
LADY PLYANT, *insolent to her husband, and easy to*   Mrs. Leigh
any pretender

Chaplain, Boy, Footmen, [Musicians] and Attendants

The SCENE, A Gallery in the LORD TOUCHWOOD's House, with
Chambers adjoining

DRAMATIS PERSONAE Q2 (PERSONAE DRAMATIS Q1)
Men Q2 (Men By Q1)
Verbruggen W1 (Alexander Q1)
Women Q2 (Women By Q1)
pretender (a) one who lays claim to something without adequate grounds (b) one
who tries to win her
House, with Chambers adjoining W1 (House. The Time, from Five o'clock to
Eight in the Evening Q1; House. Q2)

Dramatis Personae. W1's word-order, and the omission of 'By' serve to produce an
orthodox format.
Touchwood. (Fig.) irascible or passionate person who easily 'takes fire.' Literally, old,
decayed wood used as tinder, suggestive of age.
Verbruggen. The nickname Alexander, for long used (as in Q1) instead of his own
surname, derived from his desire to play this famous role in Lee's *The Rival Queens.*

Brisk. (a) (as adjective) sprightly, sharp-witted, pert, 'fast' of life, smartly dressed; (b) (as noun) 'brisk' person; a gallant or fop.

Cynthia. A name used for Artemis or Diana, divine patroness of virginity and hunting; also, for the moon personified as a goddess.

with Chambers adjoining. (a) The facade of the gallery contains several doors, two of which, to the chaplain's chamber and to the lobby of Lady Touchwood's bedchamber, need to be practical; (b) one scene (IV, vi) takes place within this bedchamber. The addition of these words, in W1, and the deletion of the statement of 'Time,' remove the unjustified claim to extreme regularity implied in Q1; see Introduction, pp. xx-xxi.

THE DOUBLE-DEALER

A Comedy

Act I, Scene i

A Gallery in the LORD TOUCHWOOD'*s House*
Enter CARELESS, *crossing the stage, with his hat, gloves and*
sword in his hands; as just risen from table: MELLEFONT
following him

MELLEFONT
Ned, Ned, whither so fast? What, turned flincher! Why,
you wo' not leave us?
CARELESS
Where are the women? Pox I'm weary of guzzling, and
begin to think them the better company.
MELLEFONT
Then thy reason staggers, and thou'rt almost drunk.   5
CARELESS
No, faith, but your fools grow noisy—and if a man must
endure the noise of words without sense, I think the women
have the more musical voices, and become nonsense better.
MELLEFONT
Why, they are at the end of the gallery, retired to their tea
and scandal, according to their ancient custom after   10
dinner.—But I made a pretence to follow you, because I had
something to say to you in private, and I am not like to have
many opportunities this evening.
CARELESS
And here's this coxcomb most critically come to interrupt
you.   15

Enter BRISK

BRISK
Boys, boys, lads, where are you? What, do you give ground?

3 *Pox* Q1 (*om.* W1)   11 *to follow* W1 (of following Q1)
8 *the more* Q1 (more W1)   14 *critically* at the critical moment
9 *the* Q2 (that Q1) (sense clear)   16 play on 'give ground' as security

11 *to follow.* W1 better provides the sense evidently intended: to follow Careless, to
persuade him to return to the table.

19

Mortgage for a bottle, ha? Careless, this is your trick; you're always spoiling company by leaving it.

CARELESS

And thou art always spoiling company by coming into't.

BRISK

Pooh, ha, ha, ha, I know you envy me. Spite, proud spite,   20
by the gods! and burning envy!—I'll be judged by
Mellefont here, who gives and takes raillery better, you or I.
Pox, man, when I say you spoil company by leaving it, I
mean you leave nobody for the company to laugh at. I think
there I was with you, ha? Mellefont?   25

MELLEFONT

O' my word, Brisk, that was a home thrust, you have
silenced him.

BRISK

Oh, my dear Mellefont, let me perish, if thou art not the
soul of conversation, the very essence of wit, and spirit of
wine,—the deuce take me if there were three good things   30
said, or one understood, since thy amputation from the
body of our society.—He! I think that's pretty and
metaphorical enough: egad I could not have said it out of
thy company,—Careless, ha?

CARELESS

Hum, ay, what is't?   35

BRISK

Oh, *mon coeur*! What is't! Nay gad I'll punish you for want
of apprehension: the deuce take me if I tell you.

MELLEFONT

No, no, hang him, he has no taste,—but, dear Brisk, excuse
me, I have a little business.

CARELESS

Prithee get thee gone; thou seest we are serious.   40

---

23 *Pox* Q1 (Pshaw W1)

20-1 *Spite. . .envy.* He misquotes a famous line from Lee's *The Rival Queens*,
Alexander's 'Spite! by the Gods, proud spite! and burning envy!' (IV,i. 426).

22 *who gives and takes raillery better.* A mark of a truewit; but like Sparkish in
Wycherley's *The Country-Wife* (1675), II,i, he is failing to distinguish between
raillery in jest and flat insult.

28-30 *the soul. . .wine* A fumbled echo of the praise of the dead Rosidore (the Earl of
Rochester) as 'the Life, the Soul of Pleasure' and 'the Spirit of Wit' in Lee, *The
Princess of Cleve* (1682), I,ii. 89, 101.

30-4 *if there. . .company.* Cf. Novel in *The Plain-Dealer*: 'Nay, pry 'thee come to us,
Manly; Gad, all the fine things one sayes, in their company, are lost, without
thee' (V,ii. 317-8).

MELLEFONT

We'll come immediately, if you'll but go in, and keep up
good humour and sense in the company: prithee do, they'll
fall asleep else.

BRISK

Egad so they will—well I will, I will, gad you shall
command me from the zenith to the nadir.—But the deuce   45
take me if I say a good thing till you come.—But prithee
dear rogue, make haste, prithee make haste, I shall burst
else.—And yonder your uncle, my Lord Touchwood,
swears he'll disinherit you, and Sir Paul Plyant threatens to
disclaim you for a son-in-law, and my Lord Froth won't   50
dance at your wedding tomorrow; nor the deuce take me, I
won't write your epithalamium—and see what a condition
you're like to be brought to.

MELLEFONT

Well, I'll speak but three words, and follow you.

BRISK

Enough, enough; Careless, bring your apprehension along   55
with you.   *Exit*

CARELESS

Pert coxcomb.

MELLEFONT

Faith 'tis a good natured coxcomb, and has very
entertaining follies—you must be more humane to him; at
this juncture it will do me service.—I'll tell you, I would   60
have mirth continued this day at any rate; though patience
purchase folly, and attention be paid with noise. There are
times when sense may be unreasonable, as well as truth.
Prithee do thou wear none today; but allow Brisk to have
wit, that thou may'st seem a fool.   65

CARELESS

Why, how now, why this extravagant proposition?

MELLEFONT

Oh, I would have no room for serious design, for I am
jealous of a plot. I would have noise and impertinence keep
my Lady Touchwood's head from working: for hell is not

48 *yonder* Q1 (yonder's W2)
68 *jealous* suspicious

62-3 *There. . .truth.* Cf. Seneca: '*The thing was true; but all Truths are not to be
spoken at all times;. . .there's no contending either with Fools, or our Superiors'*
(*Seneca's Morals by Way of Abstract,* transl. and ed. R. L'Estrange, 4th edn.
[1688], p. 168); proverb, Tilley T594 ('All truths must not be told').

more busy than her brain, nor contains more devils than   70
that imaginations.

CARELESS

I thought your fear of her had been over—is not tomorrow
appointed for your marriage with Cynthia, and her father,
Sir Paul Plyant, come to settle the writings this day, on
purpose?   75

MELLEFONT

True, but you shall judge whether I have not reason to be
alarmed. None besides you and Maskwell are acquainted
with the secret of my Aunt Touchwood's violent passion for
me. Since my first refusal of her addresses, she has
endeavoured to do me all ill offices with my uncle; yet has   80
managed 'em with that subtlety that to him they have borne
the face of kindness; while her malice, like a dark lantern,
only shone upon me, where it was directed. Still it gave me
less perplexity to prevent the success of her displeasure,
than to avoid the importunities of her love; and of two evils,   85
I thought myself favoured in her aversion: but whether
urged by her despair, and the short prospect of time she saw
to accomplish her designs; whether the hopes of revenge, or
of her love, terminated in the view of this my marriage with
Cynthia, I know not; but this morning she surprised me in   90
my bed.—

CARELESS

Was there ever such a fury? 'Tis well Nature has not put it
into her sex's power to ravish.—Well, bless us! Proceed.
What followed?

MELLEFONT

What at first amazed me; for I looked to have seen her in all   95
the transports of a slighted and revengeful woman: but
when I expected thunder from her voice, and lightning in
her eyes, I saw her melted into tears, and hushed into a sigh.
It was long before either of us spoke, passion had tied her
tongue, and amazement mine.—In short, the consequence   100
was thus, she omitted nothing that the most violent love
could urge, or tender words express; which when she saw
had no effect, but still I pleaded honour and nearness of
blood to my uncle, then came the storm I feared at first: for
starting from my bedside like a fury, she flew to my sword,   105

71 *imaginations* plots, devisings
74 *writings* documents relative to a marriage contract or settlement
88 *revenge* Q2 (her revenge Q1)
92 *put it* Q2 (put Q1)

and with much ado I prevented her doing me or herself a
mischief: having disarmed her, in a gust of passion she left
me, and in a resolution, confirmed by a thousand curses,
not to close her eyes, till she had seen my ruin.

CARELESS

Exquisite woman! But what the devil, does she think thou   110
hast no more sense than to get an heir upon her body to
disinherit thyself? For as I take it this settlement upon you
is with a proviso, that your uncle have no children.

MELLEFONT

It is so. Well, the service you are to do to me, will be a
pleasure to yourself; I must get you to engage my Lady   115
Plyant all this evening, that my pious aunt may not work
her to her interest. And if you chance to secure her to
yourself, you may incline her to mine. She's handsome, and
knows it; is very silly, and thinks she has sense, and has an
old, fond husband.   120

CARELESS

I confess a very fair foundation for a lover to build upon.

MELLEFONT

For my Lord Froth, he and his wife will be sufficiently
taken up with admiring one another, and Brisk's gallantry,
as they call it. I'll observe my uncle myself; and Jack
Maskwell has promised me, to watch my aunt narrowly,   125
and give me notice upon any suspicion. As for Sir Paul, my
wise father-in-law that is to be, my dear Cynthia has such a
share in his fatherly fondness, he would scarce make her a
moment uneasy, to have her happy hereafter.

CARELESS

So, you have manned your works: but I wish you may not   130
have the weakest guard where the enemy is strongest.

MELLEFONT

Maskwell, you mean; prithee why should you suspect him?

CARELESS

Faith I cannot help it, you know I never liked him; I am a
little superstitious in physiognomy.

MELLEFONT

He has obligations of gratitude to bind him to me; his   135
dependence upon my uncle is through my means.

CARELESS

Upon your aunt, you mean.

114 *you* W1 (that you Q1)
120 *fond* foolish; infatuated
126 *any* Q1, W2 (a Q2, W1)

MELLEFONT

My aunt!

CARELESS

I'm mistaken if there be not a familiarity between them you
do not suspect, notwithstanding her passion for you.   140

MELLEFONT

Pooh, pooh, nothing in the world but his design to do me
service; and he endeavours to be well in her esteem, that he
may be able to effect it.

CARELESS

Well, I shall be glad to be mistaken; but your aunt's
aversion in her revenge cannot be any way so effectually   145
shown, as in bringing forth a child to disinherit you. She is
handsome and cunning, and naturally wanton. Maskwell is
flesh and blood at best, and opportunities between them are
frequent. His affection to you, you have confessed, is
grounded upon his interest; that you have transplanted; and   150
should it take root in my lady, I don't see what you can
expect from the fruit.

MELLEFONT

I confess the consequence is visible, were your suspicions
just,—but see, the company is broke up, let's meet 'em.

Enter LORD TOUCHWOOD, LORD FROTH, SIR PAUL PLYANT *and*
BRISK

LORD TOUCHWOOD

Out upon't nephew—leave your father-in-law and me to   155
maintain our ground against young people.

MELLEFONT

I beg your lordship's pardon.—We were just returning.—

SIR PAUL

Were you, son? Gadsbud much better as it is—good,
strange! I swear I'm almost tipsy—t'other bottle would have
been too powerful for me,—as sure as can be it would.—We   160
wanted your company, but Mr. Brisk—where is he? I swear
and vow, he's a most facetious person—and the best
company.—And, my Lord Froth, your lordship is so merry
a man, he, he, he!

140 *notwithstanding* W1 (for all Q1)
158 *Gadsbud* God's bud (the infant Saviour)
159-60 *have been* Q1, W1 (be Q2)
162 *facetious* witty, humorous

---

140 *notwithstanding.* This gives a clearer sense than Q1's 'for all.'

LORD FROTH

Oh foy, Sir Paul, what do you mean? Merry! Oh barbarous! 165
I'd as lief you called me fool.

SIR PAUL

Nay, I protest and vow now, 'tis true; when Mr. Brisk
jokes, your lordship's laugh does so become you, he, he, he!

LORD FROTH

Ridiculous! Sir Paul, you're strangely mistaken, I find
champagne is powerful. I assure you, Sir Paul, I laugh at 170
nobody's jest but my own, or a lady's; I assure you, Sir
Paul.

BRISK

How? How, my lord? What, affront my wit! Let me perish,
do I never say anything worthy to be laughed at?

LORD FROTH

Oh foy, don't misapprehend me, I don't say so, for I often 175
smile at your conceptions. But there is nothing more
unbecoming a man of quality than to laugh; Jesu, 'tis such a
vulgar expression of the passion! Everybody can laugh.
Then especially to laugh at the jest of an inferior person, or
when anybody else of the same quality does not laugh with 180
one. Ridiculous! To be pleased with what pleases the
crowd! Now when I laugh, I always laugh alone.

BRISK

I suppose that's because you laugh at your own jests, egad,
ha, ha, ha.

LORD FROTH

He, he, I swear though, your raillery provokes me to a 185
smile.

BRISK

Ay, my lord, it's a sign I hit you in the teeth, if you show
'em.

LORD FROTH

He, he, he, I swear that's so very pretty, I can't forbear.

CARELESS

I find a quibble bears more sway in your lordship's face 190
than a jest.

---

165 *foy* ex. French, *foi*
177 *Jesu* Q1 (*om.* Q2)
181 *one* Q2 (him Q1)
187 *hit. . .teeth* retort upon you effectively
190 *quibble* pun

---

181 *one.* Q1's 'him' is manifestly awkward.
181-2 *To be. . .crowd.* Cf. Ecclesiastes, 7:3; Seneca, *De Vita Beata*, 2:2.

LORD TOUCHWOOD

Sir Paul, if you please we'll retire to the ladies, and drink a
dish of tea, to settle our heads.

SIR PAUL

With all my heart.—Mr. Brisk you'll come to us,—or call
me when you joke, I'll be ready to laugh incontinently.   195
                    Exeunt LORD TOUCHWOOD *and* SIR PAUL

MELLEFONT

But does your lordship never see comedies?

LORD FROTH

Oh yes, sometimes,—but I never laugh.

MELLEFONT

No?

LORD FROTH

Oh, no.—Never laugh indeed, sir.

CARELESS

No! Why what d'ye go there for?   200

LORD FROTH

To distinguish myself from the commonalty, and mortify
the poets; the fellows grow so conceited, when any of their
foolish wit prevails upon the side-boxes.—I swear,—he, he,
he, I have often constrained my inclinations to laugh,—he,
he, he, to avoid giving them encouragement.   205

MELLEFONT

You are cruel to yourself, my lord, as well as malicious to
them.

LORD FROTH

I confess, I did myself some violence at first, but now I
think I have conquered it.

BRISK

Let me perish, my lord, but there is something very   210
particular in the humour; 'tis true, it makes against wit, and

195 *you joke* W1 (you're going to joke Q1)
195 *incontinently* immediately; without self-restraint
200 *d'ye* Q2 (d'ee Q1)
211 *particular* Q2 (particular and novel Q1)

195 *you joke.* W1's reading has the merits of economy and elegance.
197 *never laugh.* He may vaguely recollect Seneca's praise of the stoic who vows 'As
    for me, I shall look upon death or a comedy with the same expression of
    countenance' (*De Vita Beata,* 20:3 [Loeb]). But cf. Molière, *La Critique de
    l'École des Femmes,* scene 5, noted by Kenneth Muir as the source for this
    sequence (*The Comedy of Manners* [1970], p. 105n).
203 *side-boxes.* At stage-level, and extending to the sides of the stage, these were the
    favoured resort of fashionable ladies and fops.
211 *particular.* Special, remarkable. Q2's reading has economy and elegance.

I'm sorry for some friends of mine that write, but—egad, I
love to be malicious.—Nay, deuce take me, there's wit in't
too—and wit must be foiled by wit; cut a diamond with a
diamond; no other way, egad.   215

LORD FROTH

Oh, I thought you would not be long before you found out
the wit.

CARELESS

Wit! In what? Where the devil's the wit, in not laughing
when a man has a mind to't.

BRISK

Oh Lord, why can't you find it out?—Why there 'tis, in the   220
not laughing—don't you apprehend me?—My lord,
Careless is a very honest fellow, but hark'ee,—you
understand me, somewhat heavy, a little shallow, or
so.—Why I'll tell you now, suppose now you come up to
me—nay, prithee Careless be instructed. Suppose, as I was   225
saying, you come up to me, holding your sides, and
laughing as if you would bepiss yourself—I look grave, and
ask the cause of this immoderate mirth.—You laugh on still,
and are not able to tell me—still I look grave, not so much as
smile.—   230

CARELESS

Smile, no, what the devil should you smile at, when you
suppose I can't tell you?

BRISK

Pshaw, pshaw, prithee don't interrupt me.—But I tell you,
you shall tell me—at last—but it shall be a great while first.

CARELESS

Well, but prithee don't let it be a great while, because I long   235
to have it over.

BRISK

Well then, you tell me some good jest, or very witty thing,
laughing all the while as if you were ready to die—and I
hear it, and look thus.—Would not you be disappointed?

CARELESS

No; for if it were a witty thing, I should not expect you to   240
understand it.

LORD FROTH

Oh foy, Mr. Careless, all the world allows Mr. Brisk to have

227 *bepiss yourself*—Q1 (—well—W1)
242 *allows* W1 (allow Q1)

242 *allows.* W1 correctly uses the singular verb.

wit; my wife says he has a great deal. I hope you think her a judge.

BRISK

Pooh, my lord, his voice goes for nothing.—I can't tell how 245
to make him apprehend.—Take it t'other way. Suppose I say a witty thing to you?

CARELESS

Then I shall be disappointed indeed.

MELLEFONT

Let him alone, Brisk, he is obstinately bent not to be instructed.   250

BRISK

I'm sorry for him, deuce take me.

MELLEFONT

Shall we go to the ladies, my lord?

LORD FROTH

With all my heart, methinks we are a solitude without 'em.

MELLEFONT

Or, what say you to another bottle of champagne?

LORD FROTH

Oh, for the universe, not a drop more I beseech you. Oh 255
intemperate! I have a flushing in my face already.

                    Takes out a pocket-glass, and looks in it

BRISK

Let me see, let me see, my lord, I broke my glass that was in the lid of my snuff-box. Hum! Deuce take me, I have encouraged a pimple here too.   *Takes the glass and looks*

LORD FROTH

Then you must mortify him with a patch; my wife shall 260
supply you. Come, gentlemen, *allons*, here is company coming.   *Exeunt*

[Act I, Scene ii]

Enter LADY TOUCHWOOD *and* MASKWELL

LADY TOUCHWOOD

I'll hear no more.—Y'are false and ungrateful; come, I know you false.

---

251 *deuce* Q1 (the deuce Q2)   260 *mortify* neutralise its effect
259 *encouraged* allowed to develop   261-2 *here is company coming* W1 (*not in* Q1)

261-2 *here is company coming.* W1's addition provides *liaison de vue*, to link this
   sequence with the next in neoclassical continuity.

0.1 [*I,ii*]. The scene-division is introduced here, as in Acts IV and V, when the
   stage is momentarily empty, to give some indication of dramatic structure; see
   Introduction, p. xxxviii.

MASKWELL

I have been frail, I confess, madam, for your ladyship's
service.

LADY TOUCHWOOD

That I should trust a man, whom I had known betray his   5
friend!

MASKWELL

What friend have I betrayed? Or to whom?

LADY TOUCHWOOD

Your fond friend Mellefont, and to me; can you deny it?

MASKWELL

I do not.

LADY TOUCHWOOD

Have you not wronged my lord, who has been a father to   10
you in your wants, and given you being? Have you not
wronged him in the highest manner, in his bed?

MASKWELL

With your ladyship's help, and for your service, as I told
you before. I can't deny that neither.—Anything more,
madam?   15

LADY TOUCHWOOD

More! Audacious villain. Oh, what's more is most my
shame,—have you not dishonoured me?

MASKWELL

No, that I deny; for I never told in all my life: so that
accusation's answered; on to the next.

LADY TOUCHWOOD

Death, do you dally with my passion? Insolent devil! But   20
have a care,—provoke me not; for by the eternal fire, you
shall not scape my vengeance.—Calm villain! How
unconcerned he stands, confessing treachery and
ingratitude! Is there a vice more black!—Oh I have excuses,
thousands, for my faults: fire in my temper, passions in my 25
soul, apt to every provocation; oppressed at once with love
and with despair. But a sedate, a thinking villain, whose
black blood runs temperately bad, what excuse can clear?
One who is no more moved with the reflection of his crimes
than of his face; but walks unstartled from the mirror, and 30
straight forgets the hideous form.

24 *a vice* Q2 (vice Q1)   29-31 *One. . .form* Q1 (*om.* W1)

29-31 *One. . .form.* Catoptromancy, the practice of divination by mirrors to reveal
the presence of spirits or shapes from another world, is discussed by Aubrey
Williams: Maskwell may see reflected either himself as a demon, or the demon
that possesses him (Williams, pp. 135-8). Cf. IV, vi. 58-9.

MASKWELL

Will you be in temper, madam? I would not talk not to be
heard. (*She walks about disordered*) I have been a very great
rogue for your sake, and you reproach me with it; I am
ready to be a rogue still, to do you service, and you are   35
flinging conscience and honour in my face, to rebate my
inclinations. How am I to behave myself? You know I am
your creature, my life and fortune in your power; to
disoblige you brings me certain ruin. Allow it, I would
betray you, I would not be a traitor to myself: I don't   40
pretend to honesty, because you know I am a rascal: but I
would convince you, from the necessity of my being firm to
you.

LADY TOUCHWOOD

Necessity, impudence! Can no gratitude incline you, no
obligations touch you? Have not my fortune and my person   45
been subjected to your pleasure? Were you not in the nature
of a servant, and have not I in effect made you lord of all, of
me, and of my lord? Where is that humble love, the
languishing, that adoration, which once was paid me, and
everlastingly engaged?   50

MASKWELL

Fixed, rooted in my heart, whence nothing can remove 'em,
yet you—

LADY TOUCHWOOD

Yet, what yet?

MASKWELL

Nay, misconceive me not, madam, when I say I have had a
generous and a faithful passion, which you had never   55
favoured, but through revenge and policy.

LADY TOUCHWOOD

Ha!

MASKWELL

Look you, madam, we are alone,—pray contain yourself,
and hear me. You know you loved your nephew, when I
first sighed for you; I quickly found it, an argument that I   60
loved; for with that art you veiled your passion, 'twas

32 *in temper* temperate
36 *rebate* lessen, make dull

---

33 S.D. This placement is less distracting than having it between 'been' and 'a', as
in Q1, where this occurs simply through the lineation of the dialogue in relation
to the indented S.D.
60 *found it.* Either 'perceived it to be' or 'found it out, (which was)' (*OED*, 5,8).

imperceptible to all but jealous eyes. This discovery made
me bold; I confess it; for by it I thought you in my power.
Your nephew's scorn of you added to my hopes; I watched
the occasion, and took you, just repulsed by him, warm at   65
once with love and indignation; your disposition, my
arguments, and happy opportunity, accomplished my
design; I pressed the yielding minute, and was blest. How I
have loved you since, words have not shown, then how
should words express?   70

LADY TOUCHWOOD
Well, mollifying devil!—And have I not met your love with
forward fire?

MASKWELL
Your zeal I grant was ardent, but misplaced; there was
revenge in view; that woman's idol had defiled the temple
of the god, and love was made a mock-worship.—A son and   75
heir would have edged young Mellefont upon the brink of
ruin, and left him none but you to catch at for prevention.

LADY TOUCHWOOD
Again, provoke me! Do you wind me like a larum, only to
rouse my own stilled soul for your diversion? Confusion!

MASKWELL
Nay, madam, I'm gone, if you relapse,—what needs this? I   80
say nothing but what yourself, in open hours of love, have
told me. Why should you deny it? Nay, how can you? Is not
all this present heat owing to the same fire? Do you not love
him still? How have I this day offended you, but in not
breaking off his match with Cynthia? Which ere tomorrow   85
shall be done,—had you but patience.

LADY TOUCHWOOD
How, what said you, Maskwell,—another caprice to unwind
my temper?

77 *none* Q2 (nought Q1)
78 *larum* apparatus attached to clock or watch, to produce ringing sound
81 *yourself* Q1 (you yourself W1)
82 *you?* Q1 (you deny it? W2)

74-5 *that. . .mock-worship.* 'Your soul (or, heart), as a temple dedicated to the
worship of your lover, myself, has been defiled by the introduction of an idol,
revenge, to which your true worship is given,' etc. (cf. 2 Kings, 21:4-7; 1
Corinthians, 3:17; 2 Corinthians, 6:16). That 'Revenge is womanish' was
proverbial (Tilley R91); cf. Juvenal, Satire XIII, ll. 191-2.
77 *none.* Q1's 'nought' relegates her to the status of an object.
81 *yourself.* Q1's reading involves the substitution of 'yourself' for 'you,' described
in *OED* as archaic and poetic.

MASKWELL

By heaven, no; I am your slave, the slave of all your
pleasures; and will not rest till I have given you peace,   90
would you suffer me.

LADY TOUCHWOOD

Oh Maskwell, in vain I do disguise me from thee, thou
knowest me, knowest the very inmost windings and recesses
of my soul.—Oh Mellefont! I burn; married tomorrow!
Despair strikes me. Yet my soul knows I hate him too: let   95
him but once be mine, and next immediate ruin seize him.

MASKWELL

Compose yourself. You shall enjoy and ruin him too,—will
that please you?

LADY TOUCHWOOD

How, how? Thou dear, thou precious villain, how?

MASKWELL

You have already been tampering with my Lady Plyant?   100

LADY TOUCHWOOD

I have: she is ready for any impression I think fit.

MASKWELL

She must be throughly persuaded that Mellefont loves her.

LADY TOUCHWOOD

She is so credulous that way naturally, and likes him so
well, that she will believe it faster than I can persuade her.
But I don't see what you can propose from such a trifling   105
design; for her first conversing with Mellefont will
convince her of the contrary.

MASKWELL

I know it.—I don't depend upon it.—But it will prepare
something else, and gain us leisure to lay a stronger plot: if I
gain a little time, I shall not want contrivance.   110
          One minute gives invention to destroy
          What, to rebuild, will a whole age employ.
                                        Exeunt

97 *enjoy* Q1 (possess W1)
102 *throughly* Q1 (thoroughly W2)

111-2 Cf. 'An hour may destroy what an age was a-building' (Fuller, *Gnomologia*
[1732]); Tilley M265.

Act II

[The Gallery]
Enter LADY FROTH *and* CYNTHIA

CYNTHIA

Indeed, madam! Is it possible your ladyship could have
been so much in love?

LADY FROTH

I could not sleep; I did not sleep one wink for three weeks
together.

CYNTHIA

Prodigious! I wonder, want of sleep, and so much love, and   5
so much wit as your ladyship has, did not turn your brain.

LADY FROTH

Oh my dear Cynthia, you must not rally your friend,—but
really, as you say, I wonder too,—but then I had a way. For
between you and I, I had whimsies and vapours, but I gave
them vent.   10

CYNTHIA

How pray, madam?

LADY FROTH

Oh I writ, writ abundantly,—do you never write?

CYNTHIA

Write, what?

LADY FROTH

Songs, elegies, satires, encomiums, panegyrics, lampoons,
plays, or heroic poems.   15

CYNTHIA

Oh Lord, not I, madam; I'm content to be a courteous
reader.

LADY FROTH

Oh inconsistent! In love, and not write! If my lord and I had
been both of your temper, we had never come together,—oh
bless me! What a sad thing would that have been, if my lord   20
and I should never have met!

CYNTHIA

Then neither my lord nor you would ever have met with
your match, on my conscience.

3 *not sleep; I did not* Q1 (*om.* W2)
9 *whimsies* capricious humours; dizzinesses
22 *nor* Q2 (and Q1)
22 *ever* Q1, W1 (never Q2)
22-3 *met with your match* proverbial, Tilley M745

22 *nor.* The construction was initially confused.

LADY FROTH

O' my conscience no more we should; thou sayest right—for
sure my Lord Froth is as fine a gentleman, and as much a   25
man of quality! Ah! Nothing at all of the common air,—I
think I may say he wants nothing, but a blue ribbon and a
star, to make him shine the very phosphorus of our
hemisphere. Do you understand those two hard words? If
you don't, I'll explain 'em to you.   30

CYNTHIA

Yes, yes, madam, I'm not so ignorant.—(*Aside*) At least I
won't own it, to be troubled with your instructions.

LADY FROTH

Nay, I beg your pardon, but being derived from the Greek,
I thought you might have escaped the etymology.—But I'm
the more amazed, to find you a woman of letters, and not   35
write! Bless me! How can Mellefont believe you love him?

CYNTHIA

Why faith, madam, he that won't take my word, shall never
have it under my hand.

LADY FROTH

I vow Mellefont's a pretty gentleman, but methinks he
wants a manner.   40

CYNTHIA

A manner! What's that, madam?

LADY FROTH

Some distinguishing quality, as for example, the *bel air* or
brillant of Mr. Brisk; the solemnity, yet complaisance of my
lord; or something of his own, that should look a little *je -ne-
sais-quoi*-ish; he is too much a mediocrity, in my mind.   45

CYNTHIA

He does not indeed affect either pertness or formality, for
which I like him: here he comes.

LADY FROTH

And my lord with him: pray observe the difference.

27-8 *a blue ribbon and a star* insignia of the Order of the Garter
28 *phosphorus* morning-star
29 *hemisphere* half of the celestial sphere, esp. that part of the heavens seen above
the horizon
44-5 *je-ne-sais-quoi-ish* Ed. (*jene-scay-quoysh* Q1)

44-5 *je-ne-sais-quoi-ish*. The *je ne sais quoi*, i.e., 'The secret charm, or the
unexpressible somewhat. . .consists in a certain taking air, in an agreeableness
that hath no name but which is seen in speaking, in the ways of acting, and in
reasoning' (Balthazar Gracian, *The Courtier's Manual Oracle, or, the Art of
Prudence,* transl. [1685], pp. 117-8).

Enter LORD FROTH, MELLEFONT, BRISK

CYNTHIA (*Aside*)
  Impertinent creature, I could almost be angry with her
  now.   50

LADY FROTH
  My lord, I have been telling Cynthia how much I have been
  in love with you; I swear I have; I'm not ashamed to own it
  now; ah! It makes my heart leap, I vow I sigh when I think
  on't: my dear lord! Ha, ha, ha, do you remember, my lord?
            Squeezes him by the hand, looks kindly on him, sighs
                                            and then laughs out

LORD FROTH
  Pleasant creature! Perfectly well; ah! That look, ay, there it   55
  is, who could resist? 'Twas so my heart was made a captive
  first, and ever since 't has been in love with happy slavery.

LADY FROTH
  Oh that tongue, that dear, deceitful tongue! That charming
  softness in your mien and your expression, and then your
  bow! Good my lord, bow as you did when I gave you my   60
  picture, here suppose this my picture.— (*Gives him a
  pocket-glass*) Pray mind my lord; ah! He bows charmingly;
  nay, my lord, you shan't kiss it so much; I shall grow
  jealous, I vow now.
            He bows profoundly low, then kisses the glass

LORD FROTH
  I saw myself there, and kissed it for your sake.   65

LADY FROTH
  Ah! Gallantry to the last degree—Mr. Brisk, you're a judge;
  was ever anything so well-bred as my lord?

BRISK
  Never anything; but your ladyship, let me perish.

LADY FROTH
  Oh prettily turned again; let me die but you have a great
  deal of wit: Mr. Mellefont, don't you think Mr. Brisk has a   70
  world of wit?

MELLEFONT
  Oh yes, madam.

BRISK
  Oh Lord, madam—

---

51 *Cynthia* Q2 (my dear Cynthia Q1)
73 *Lord* Q1 (dear W1)

---

51 *Cynthia.* Q2 has a crisper rhythm and focus.

LADY FROTH
An infinite deal!

BRISK
Oh Jesu, madam—   75

LADY FROTH
More wit than anybody.

BRISK
I'm everlastingly your humble servant, deuce take me,
madam.

LORD FROTH
Don't you think us a happy couple?

CYNTHIA
I vow, my lord, I think you the happiest couple in the   80
world, for you're not only happy in one another, and when
you are together, but happy in yourselves, and by
yourselves.

LORD FROTH
I hope Mellefont will make a good husband too.

CYNTHIA
'Tis my interest to believe he will, my lord.   85

LORD FROTH
D'ye think he'll love you as well as I do my wife? I'm afraid
not.

CYNTHIA
I believe he'll love me better.

LORD FROTH
Heavens! That can never be; but why do you think so?

CYNTHIA
Because he has not so much reason to be fond of himself.   90

LORD FROTH
Oh your humble servant for that, dear madam; well,
Mellefont, you'll be a happy creature.

MELLEFONT
Ay, my lord, I shall have the same reason for my happiness
that your lordship has, I shall think myself happy.

LORD FROTH
Ah, that's all.   95

BRISK (*To* LADY FROTH)
Your ladyship is in the right; but egad I'm wholly turned

---

75 *Jesu* Q1 (heav'ns Q2)
81 *you're* Q2 (you are Q1)

---

81 *you're.* Q2's alteration achieves greater economy and colloquial force.

into satire. I confess I write but seldom, but when I
do—keen iambics, egad. But my lord was telling me your
ladyship has made an essay toward an heroic poem.

LADY FROTH

Did my lord tell you? Yes I vow, and the subject is my   100
lord's love to me. And what do you think I call it? I dare
swear you won't guess—*The Sillibub*, ha, ha, ha.

BRISK

Because my lord's title's Froth, egad, ha, ha, ha, deuce take
me, very apropos and surprising, ha, ha, ha.

LADY FROTH

He, ay, is not it?—and then I call my lord *Spumoso*; and   105
myself, what d'ye think I call myself?

BRISK

Lactilla, maybe,—'gad I cannot tell.

LADY FROTH

Biddy, that's all, just my own name.

BRISK

Biddy! Egad very pretty—deuce take me if your ladyship
has not the art of surprising the most naturally in the   110
world,—I hope you'll make me happy in communicating
the poem.

LADY FROTH

Oh, you must be my confidant, I must ask your advice.

BRISK

I'm your humble servant, let me perish,—I presume your
ladyship has read Bossu?   115

LADY FROTH

Oh yes, and Rapine, and Dacier upon Aristotle and
Horace.—My lord, you must not be jealous, I'm
communicating all to Mr. Brisk.

---

102 *Sillibub* Q1; sillabub, dish made from milk curded with wine or cider
    (also, floridly vapid writing)

---

98 *keen iambics*. 'Horace's "celeres iambos," *Carminem*, I, xvi, 24' (Summers).

115 *Bossu*. René le Bossu (1631-80), 'a French critic of much authority in his day'
    (Summers). His *Traité du Poésie Épique* (Paris, 1975) was not translated into
    English until 1695.

116 *Rapine*. René Rapine (1621-87), whose main critical work (Paris, 1674-5) was
    translated as *Reflections on Aristotle's Treatise of Poesie* by Thomas Rymer,
    1674-5.

116-7 *Dacier*. André Dacier (1651-1722), author of *Remarques Critiques sur les
    Oeuvres d'Horace*, 10 vols. (Paris, 1681) and *La Poétique d' Aristote Traduite en
    François* (Paris, 1692). 'A French scholar of much repute' (Summers).

LORD FROTH

No, no, I'll allow Mr. Brisk; have you nothing about you to
show him, my dear?   120

LADY FROTH

Yes, I believe I have.—Mr. Brisk, come, will you go into the
next room? And there I'll show you all I have.

Exeunt LADY FROTH *and* BRISK

LORD FROTH

I'll walk a turn in the garden, and come to you.   *Exit*

MELLEFONT

You're thoughtful, Cynthia?

CYNTHIA

I'm thinking, though marriage makes man and wife one   125
flesh, it leaves 'em still two fools; and they become more
conspicuous by setting off one another.

MELLEFONT

That's only when two fools meet, and their follies are
opposed.

CYNTHIA

Nay, I have known two wits meet, and by the opposition of 130
their wit, render themselves as ridiculous as fools. 'Tis an
odd game we're going to play at: what think you of drawing
stakes, and giving over in time?

MELLEFONT

No, hang't, that's not endeavouring to win, because it's
possible we may lose; since we have shuffled and cut, let's 135
e'en turn up trump now.

CYNTHIA

Then I find it's like cards, if either of us have a good hand it
is an accident of fortune.

MELLEFONT

No, marriage is rather like a game of bowls: Fortune indeed
makes the match, and the two nearest and sometimes the   140
two farthest are together, but the game depends entirely
upon judgement.

---

122 *all* Q1 (what Q2)
125 *though* Q2 (that though Q1)
131 *wit* W1 (wits Q1)

---

125 *though.* Q1's 'that though' is unconcise and uneuphonious.
131 *wit.* Q1's 'wits' creates confusion with the subject, 'two wits.'
131-46 Comparisons of wooing to a game, expecially of bowls, were a recognized
   exercise of wit; cf. John Day, *The Isle of Gulls* (1606), sigs. E1-E2; William
   Mountfort, *Greenwich Park* (1691), p. 20.

CYNTHIA

Still it is a game, and consequently one of us must be a
loser.

MELLEFONT

Not at all; only a friendly trial of skill, and the winnings to   145
be laid out in an entertainment.—What's here, the music?—
                              (MUSICIANS *crossing the stage*)
Oh, my lord has promised the company a new song, we'll
get 'em to give it us by the way. [*To the* MUSICIANS] Pray let
us have the favour of you to practise the song, before the
company hear it.   150

SONG

Cynthia frowns whene'er I woo her,
Yet she's vexed if I give over;
Much she fears I should undo her,
But much more to lose her lover:
Thus, in doubting, she refuses;   155
And not winning, thus she loses.

Prithee Cynthia look behind you,
Age and wrinkles will o'ertake you;
Then too late desire will find you,
When the power must forsake you: 160
Think, oh think, o' th' sad condition,
To be past, yet wish fruition.

MELLEFONT (*To the* MUSICIANS)

You shall have my thanks below.   *They go out*

Enter SIR PAUL PLYANT *and* LADY PLYANT

SIR PAUL

Gadsbud! I am provoked into a fermentation, as my Lady
Froth says; was ever the like read of in story?   165

146 *laid out in an entertainment* W1 (shared between us Q1)
146 *music* musicians
146.1 MUSICIANS. . .*stage*. S.D. so placed *Ewald* (*follows* way, Q1; *follows*
        entertainment, *Bateson*)
160 *must* W1 (does Q1)

_____

146 *laid out in an entertainment*. W1's reading adds a new twist, suggesting their
      marriage is to produce both pleasure, and a sharing of benefits with others.
146.1 MUSICIANS. . .*stage*. Such S.D.s, often placed in the right hand margin, were
      difficult for the compositor to insert correctly. Here the entry roughly coincides
      with 'What's here. . .?'
160 *must*. This is stronger than Q1's 'does' and syntactically neater.

LADY PLYANT

Sir Paul have patience, let me alone to rattle him up.

SIR PAUL

Pray your ladyship give me leave to be angry—I'll rattle
him up I warrant you, I'll firk him with a *certiorari*.

LADY PLYANT

You firk him! I'll firk him myself; pray Sir Paul hold you
contented.   170

CYNTHIA [*To* MELLEFONT]

Bless me, what makes my father in such a passion?—I never
saw him thus before.

SIR PAUL

Hold yourself contented, my Lady Plyant,—I find passion
coming upon me by inspiration, and I cannot submit as
formerly, therefore give way.   175

LADY PLYANT

How now! Will you be pleased to retire, and—

SIR PAUL

No marry will I not be pleased, I am pleased to be angry,
that's my pleasure at this time.

MELLEFONT

What can this mean?

LADY PLYANT

Gads my life, the man's distracted; why how now, who are   180
you? What am I? 'Slidikins can't I govern you? What did I
marry you for? Am I not to be absolute and uncontrollable?
Is it fit a woman of my spirit and conduct should be
contradicted in a matter of this concern?

SIR PAUL

It concerns me, and only me;—besides, I'm not to be   185
governed at all times. When I am in tranquillity, my Lady
Plyant shall command Sir Paul; but when I am provoked to
fury, I cannot incorporate with patience and reason,—as
soon may tigers match with tigers, lambs with lambs, and
every creature couple with its foe, as the poet says.—   190

LADY PLYANT

He's hot-headed still! 'Tis in vain to talk to you; but

---

168 *firk* chastise   181 *'Slidikins* ex. God's lid
168 *certiorari* legal writ   188 *incorporate* unite or combine
174 *inspiration* Q1 (inflation W1)   with (also, copulate)

188-90 *the poet*. i.e., Horace, in *Ars Poetica*, 12-13: poetic licence may be claimed,
    and granted, 'but not so far that savage should match with tame, or serpents
    couple with birds, lambs with tigers' (Loeb).

remember I have a curtain-lecture for you, you disobedient, headstrong brute.

SIR PAUL

No, 'tis because I won't be headstrong, because I won't be a brute, and have my head fortified, that I am thus 195 exasperated,—but I will protect my honour, and yonder is the violator of my fame.

LADY PLYANT

'Tis my honour that is concerned, and the violation was intended to me. Your honour! You have none but what is in my keeping, and I can dispose of it when I please—therefore 200 don't provoke me.

SIR PAUL

Hum, gadsbud she says true,—well, my lady, march on, I will fight under you then: I am convinced, as far as passion will permit.

LADY PLYANT *and* SIR PAUL *come up to* MELLEFONT

LADY PLYANT

Inhuman and treacherous.—   205

SIR PAUL

Thou serpent and first tempter of womankind.—

CYNTHIA

Bless me! Sir; madam; what mean you?

SIR PAUL

Thy, Thy, come away, Thy, touch him not, come hither, girl, go not near him, there's nothing but deceit about him; snakes are in his peruke, and the crocodile of *Nilus* in his 210 belly, he will eat thee up alive.

LADY PLYANT

Dishonourable, impudent creature!

MELLEFONT

For heaven's sake, madam, to whom do you direct this language?

LADY PLYANT

Have I behaved myself with all the decorum and nicety 215 befitting the person of Sir Paul's wife? Have I preserved my honour as it were in a snow-house for this three year past? Have I been white and unsullied even by Sir Paul himself?

192 *curtain-lecture* reproof given in bed by wife to husband
194 *because I won't be headstrong* Q1 (*om.* W2)
195 *fortified* i.e with a cuckold's horns
210 *in* Q1 (is in W1)
217 *snow-house* house in which snow was preserved
217 *this three year* Q1 (these three years Q2)

SIR PAUL

Nay, she has been an impenetrable wife, even to me, that's
the truth on't.   220

LADY PLYANT

Have I, I say, preserved myself, like a fair sheet of paper, for
you to make a blot upon?—

SIR PAUL

And she shall make a simile with any woman in England.

MELLEFONT

I am so amazed, I know not what to speak.

SIR PAUL

Do you think my daughter, this pretty creature—gadsbud   225
she's a wife for a cherubin!—do you think her fit for nothing
but to be a stalking-horse, to stand before you while you
take aim at my wife? Gadsbud I was never angry before in
my life, and I'll never be appeased again.

MELLEFONT (*Aside*)

Hell and damnation! This is my aunt; such malice can be   230
engendered nowhere else.

LADY PLYANT

Sir Paul, take Cynthia from his sight; leave me to strike him
with the remorse of his intended crime.

CYNTHIA

Pray, sir, stay, hear him, I dare affirm he's innocent.

SIR PAUL

Innocent! Why hark'ee, come hither Thy, hark'ee, I had it   235
from his aunt, my sister Touchwood,—gadsbud he does not
care a farthing for anything of thee, but thy portion; why,
he's in love with my wife; he would have tantalized thee,
and made a cuckold of thy poor father,—and that would
certainly have broke my heart—I'm sure if ever I should   240
have horns, they would kill me; they would never come
kindly, I should die of 'em, like any child that were cutting
his teeth—I should, indeed, Thy—therefore come away; but
Providence has prevented all, therefore come away, when I
bid you.   245

219 *impenetrable* Q1 (invincible W1)
224 *speak* Q1 (say W1)
242 *any* Q1 (a Q2)
242 *were* Q1 (was Q2)

---

221 *a fair sheet of paper*. 'Let us then suppose the mind [at birth] to be, as we say,
white paper, void of all Characters, without any *Ideas*. . .How comes it to be
furnished?. . .From *Experience*' (John Locke, *An Essay Concerning Human
Understanding* [1690], ed. P.H. Nidditch [Oxford, 1975], p. 104).

CYNTHIA

I must obey.   *Exeunt* SIR PAUL *and* CYNTHIA

LADY PLYANT

Oh, such a thing! The impiety of it startles me—to wrong so
good, so fair a creature, and one that loved you
tenderly—'tis a barbarity of barbarities, and nothing could
be guilty of it—

MELLEFONT

But the greatest villain imagination can form, I grant it; and   250
next to the villainy of such a fact is the villainy of aspersing
me with the guilt. How? Which way was I to wrong her?
For yet I understand you not.

LADY PLYANT

Why, gads my life, cousin Mellefont, you cannot be so
peremptory as to deny it, when I tax you with it to your   255
face; for now Sir Paul's gone, you are *corum nobus*.

MELLEFONT

By heaven, I love her more than life, or—

LADY PLYANT

Fiddle-faddle, don't tell me of this and that, and everything
in the world, but give me mathemacular demonstration,   260
answer me directly—but I have not patience—oh! The
impiety of it, as I was saying, and the unparallelled
wickedness! Oh merciful Father! How could you think to
reverse nature so, to make the daughter the means of
procuring the mother?   265

MELLEFONT

The daughter to procure the mother!

LADY PLYANT

Ay, for though I am not Cynthia's own mother, I am her
father's wife; and that's near enough to make it incest.

248 *loved* Q1 (loves W1)
252 *aspersing* injuriously and falsely charging
256 *peremptory* obstinate
257 *corum nobus* i.e. *coram nobis*, in presence of one another
263 *Oh* (*om.* W2)
266 *to procure* Q2 (procure Q1)

---

260 *mathemacular demonstration.* She recalls Thomas Rymer on *Othello* 'Thirdly,
This may be a lesson to Husbands, that before their Jealousie be Tragical, the
proofs may be Mathematical' (*A Short View of Tragedy* [1692], *The Critical
Works of Thomas Rymer*. ed. C.A. Zimansky [New Haven, 1956], p. 132).

266 *to procure.* W1's reading conveys a more accurate response: 'the daughter' has
been proposed as means not agent.

267-8 *I am. . .incest.* She will become by marriage his stepmother, hence within the
limits of forbidden affinity, as set out in *The Book of Common Prayer*.

MELLEFONT (*Aside*)

Incest! Oh my precious aunt and the devil in conjunction.

LADY PLYANT

Oh reflect upon the horror of that, and then the guilt of   270
deceiving everybody; marrying the daughter, only to make
a cuckold of the father; and then seducing me, debauching
my purity, and perverting me from the road of virtue, in
which I have trod thus long, and never made one trip, not
one *faux pas*; oh consider it, what would you have to answer   275
for, if you should provoke me to frailty? Alas! Humanity is
feeble, heaven knows! Very feeble, and unable to support
itself.

MELLEFONT

Where am I? Is it day? And am I awake? Madam—

LADY PLYANT

And nobody knows how circumstances may happen   280
together,—to my thinking, now I could resist the strongest
temptation,—but yet I know, 'tis impossible for me to know
whether I could or not, there's no certainty in the things of
this life.

MELLEFONT

Madam, pray give me leave to ask you one question.—   285

LADY PLYANT

Oh Lord, ask me the question! I'll swear I'll refuse it: I
swear I'll deny it—therefore don't ask me, nay you shan't
ask me, I swear I'll deny it. Oh Gemini, you have brought
all the blood into my face; I warrant, I am as red as a turkey-
cock; oh fie, cousin Mellefont!   290

MELLEFONT

Nay, madam, hear me; I mean—

LADY PLYANT

Hear you? No, no; I'll deny you first, and hear you
afterwards: For one does not know how one's mind may
change upon hearing—hearing is one of the senses, and all
the senses are fallible; I won't trust my honour, I assure   295
you; my honour is infallible and un-come-at-able.

---

279 *Is* W1 (Sure, is Q1)   296 *un-come-at-table Kemble* (uncomatible Q1)
283 *not* Q2 (no Q1)   ex. come at: approach, come into sexual
283 *there's* Q2 (there is Q1)   connection with
293 *afterwards* Q1 (afterward W2)

---

279 *Is.* W1 provides economy and elegance.
283 *not, there's.* Q1's 'no' involves confusion with 'no' in the following clause, and
'there is' offers a weaker speech rhythm.

MELLEFONT

For heaven's sake, madam.—

LADY PLYANT

Oh name it no more—bless me, how can you talk of heaven,
and have so much wickedness in your heart? Maybe you
don't think it a sin,—they say some of you gentlemen don't   300
think it a sin,—maybe it is no sin to them that don't think it
so;—indeed, if I did not think it a sin,—but still my honour,
if it were no sin,—but then, to marry my daughter, for the
conveniency of frequent opportunities,—I'll never consent
to that, as sure as can be, I'll break the match.   305

MELLEFONT

Death and amazement,—madam, upon my knees—[*Kneels*]

LADY PLYANT

Nay, nay, rise up, come you shall see my good nature.[*He
rises*] I know love is powerful, and nobody can help his
passion: 'tis not your fault; nor I swear it is not mine.—How
can I help it, if I have charms? And how can you help it, if   310
you are made a captive; I swear it's pity it should be a
fault,—but my honour,—well, but your honour too—but
the sin!—Well but the necessity—oh Lord, here's somebody
coming, I dare not stay. Well, you must consider of your
crime; and strive as much as can be against it,—strive be   315
sure—but don't be melancholy, don't despair,—but never
think that I'll grant you anything; oh Lord, no;—but be
sure you lay aside all thoughts of the marriage, for though I
know you don't love Cynthia, only as a blind for your
passion to me; yet it will make me jealous,—oh Lord, what   320
did I say? Jealous! No, no, I can't be jealous, for I must not
love you,—therefore don't hope,—but don't despair
neither,—oh, they're coming, I must fly.   *Exit*

MELLEFONT (*After a pause*)

So then,—spite of my care and foresight, I am caught,
caught in my security,—yet this was but a shallow artifice,   325
unworthy of my Machiavellian aunt: there must be more
behind, this is but the first flash, the priming of her engine;
destruction follows hard, if not most presently prevented.

Enter MASKWELL

Maskwell, welcome, thy presence is a view of land,

311 *it's* Q1 (it is W1)
316 *melancholy* Q1 (melancholic W1)
328 *presently* immediately, speedily

appearing to my shipwrecked hopes; the witch has raised   330
the storm, and her ministers have done their work; you see
the vessels are parted.

MASKWELL

I know it; I met Sir Paul towing away Cynthia. Come,
trouble not your head, I'll join you together ere tomorrow
morning, or drown between you in the attempt.   335

MELLEFONT

There's comfort in a hand stretched out, to one that's
sinking, though ne'er so far off.

MASKWELL

No sinking, nor no danger,—come, cheer up; why, you
don't know that while I plead for you, your aunt has given
me a retaining fee;—nay, I am your greatest enemy, and she   340
does but journey-work under me.

MELLEFONT

Ha! How's this?

MASKWELL

What d'ye think of my being employed in the execution of
all her plots? Ha, ha, ha, by heaven it's true; I have
undertaken to break the match, I have undertaken to make   345
your uncle disinherit you, to get you turned out of doors;
and to—ha, ha, ha, I can't tell you for laughing,—oh she has
opened her heart to me,—I am to turn you a-grazing, and
to—ha, ha, ha, marry Cynthia myself; there's a plot for you.

MELLEFONT

Ha! Oh see, I see my rising sun! Light breaks through   350
clouds upon me, and I shall live in day—oh my Maskwell!
How shall I thank or praise thee? Thou hast outwitted
woman.—But tell me, how couldst thou thus get into her
confidence?—Ha! How? But was it her contrivance to
persuade my Lady Plyant to this extravagant belief?   355

MASKWELL

It was, and to tell you the truth, I encouraged it for your
diversion: though it made you a little uneasy for the
present, yet the reflection of it must needs be
entertaining—I warrant she was very violent at first.

---

339 *plead* as advocate in court   350 *Oh see* Q2 (Oh I see Q1)
341 *journey-work* the work of a subordinate   358 *reflection* recollection

330-1 *the witch has raised the storm.* An activity often attributed to witches; see
    Rossell Hope Robins, *The Encyclopaedia of Witchcraft and Demonology* (8th
    printing, New York, 1970), pp. 487-9.
350 *Oh see.* Q2 lightens the repetition, and objectifies the vision.

MELLEFONT

Ha, ha, ha, ay, a very fury; but I was most afraid of her   360
violence at last,—if you had not come as you did, I don't
know what she might have attempted.

MASKWELL

Ha, ha, ha, I know her temper,—well, you must know then,
that all my contrivances were but bubbles; till at last I
pretended to have been long secretly in love with Cynthia;   365
that did my business; that convinced your aunt I might be
trusted; since it was as much my interest as hers to break the
match: then, she thought my jealousy might qualify me to
assist her in her revenge. And in short, in that belief, told
me the secrets of her heart. At length we made this   370
agreement, if I accomplish her designs (as I told you before)
she has engaged to put Cynthia with all her fortune into my
power.

MELLEFONT

She is most gracious in her favour,—well, and dear Jack,
how hast thou contrived?   375

MASKWELL

I would not have you stay to hear it now; for I don't know,
but she may come this way; I am to meet her anon; after
that I'll tell you the whole matter; be here in this gallery an
hour hence, by that time I imagine our consultation may be
over.   380

MELLEFONT

I will; till then success attend thee.   *Exit*

MASKWELL

Till then, success will attend me; for when I meet you, I
meet the only obstacle to my fortune. Cynthia, let thy
beauty gild my crimes; and whatsoever I commit of
treachery or deceit shall be imputed to me as a   385
merit.—Treachery! What treachery? Love cancels all the
bonds of friendship, and sets men right upon their first
foundations.

360 *ay* Q1 (ay, ay W2)
364 *bubbles* worthless efforts, shams
386-7 *Love. . .friendship* proverbial, Tilley L549, 'When love puts in friendship is
    gone'

387-8 *their first foundations.* i.e., in Thomas Hobbes' 'Natural condition of
    mankind,' a state of 'warre of every man against every man. . .The notions of
    Right and Wrong, Justice and Injustice have there no place. . .Force, and
    Fraud, are in warre the two Cardinall vertues' (*Leviathan,* ed. C.B. Macpherson
    [Harmondsworth, 1968], p. 188).

Duty to kings, piety to parents, gratitude to benefactors,
and fidelity to friends, are different and particular ties: but   390
the name of "rival" cuts 'em all asunder, and is a general
acquittance—rival is equal, and love like death an universal
leveller of mankind. Ha! But is there not such a thing as
honesty? Yes, and whosoever has it about him bears an
enemy in his breast: for your honest man, as I take it, is that   395
nice, scrupulous, conscientious person who will cheat
nobody but himself; such another coxcomb as your wise
man, who is too hard for all the world, and will be made a
fool of by nobody, but himself: ha, ha, ha. Well, for wisdom
and honesty, give me cunning and hypocrisy; oh 'tis such a   400
pleasure to angle for fair-faced fools! Then that hungry
gudgeon Credulity will bite at anything.—Why, let me see,
I have the same face, the same words and accents, when I
speak what I do think, and when I speak what I do not
think—the very same—and dear dissimulation is the only   405
art not to be known from nature.
    Why will mankind be fools, and be deceived?
    And why friends' and lovers' oaths believed?
    When each, who searches strictly his own mind,
    May so much fraud and power of baseness find.   410
                                                    [*Exit*]

Act III

[*The Gallery*]
Enter LORD TOUCHWOOD *and* LADY TOUCHWOOD

LADY TOUCHWOOD
    My lord, can you blame my brother Plyant, if he refuse his

392-3 *death. . .leveller* proverbial, Tilley D143, 'Death is the grand leveller'

389-92 He cynically reverses Cicero's dictum that 'To take something away from
    someone else. . .strikes at the roots of human society and fellowship. . .[for it
    demolishes] the link that unites every human being with every other' (*De
    Officiis*, III,iii, in Cicero, *Selected Works*, transl. M. Grant [Harmondsworth,
    1969], p. 166).
394-5 *an enemy in his breast*. 'An utterly malignant twist on an age-old proverb,
    Colubrum in sinu fovere   ("To bring up a snake in one's bosome, viz. to
    entertain one, thinking him to be a Friend, who afterwards proves a mortal
    Enemy")' (Williams, p. 138); Tilley V68. Cf. V, iii. 58-9.
401-2 *hungry gudgeon Credulity*. 'Owing to the gudgeon being much used for bait, the
    word came to mean a gull, one that will bite at any bait' (Summers).

daughter upon this provocation? The contract's void by this unheard-of impiety.

LORD TOUCHWOOD

I don't believe it true; he has better principles—foh, 'tis nonsense. Come, come, I know my Lady Plyant has a large   5
eye, and would centre everything in her own circle; 'tis not the first time she has mistaken respect for love, and made Sir Paul jealous of the civility of an undesigning person, the better to bespeak his security in her unfeigned pleasures.

LADY TOUCHWOOD

You censure hardly, my lord; my sister's honour is very   10
well known.

LORD TOUCHWOOD

Yes, I believe I know some that have been familiarly acquainted with it. This is a little trick wrought by some pitiful contriver, envious of my nephew's merit.

LADY TOUCHWOOD

Nay, my lord, it may be so, and I hope it will be found so: 15
but that will require some time; for in such a case as this, demonstration is necessary.

LORD TOUCHWOOD

There should have been demonstration of the contrary too, before it had been believed—

LADY TOUCHWOOD

So I suppose there was.   20

LORD TOUCHWOOD

How? Where? When?

LADY TOUCHWOOD

That I can't tell; nay, I don't say there was—I am willing to believe as favourably of my nephew as I can.

LORD TOUCHWOOD (*Half aside*)

I don't know that.

LADY TOUCHWOOD

How? Don't you believe that, say you, my lord?   25

LORD TOUCHWOOD

No, I don't say so—I confess I am troubled to find you so cold in his defence.

LADY TOUCHWOOD

His defence! Bless me, would you have me defend an ill thing?

LORD TOUCHWOOD

You believe it then?   30

LADY TOUCHWOOD

I don't know; I am very unwilling to speak my thoughts in

anything that may be to my cousin's disadvantage; besides, I find, my lord, you are prepared to receive an ill impression from any opinion of mine which is not consenting with your own: but since I am like to be 35 suspected in the end, and 'tis a pain any longer to dissemble, I own it to you; in short I do believe it, nay, and can believe anything worse, if it were laid to his charge—don't ask me my reasons, my lord, for they are not fit to be told you. 40

LORD TOUCHWOOD

(*Aside*) I'm amazed, here must be something more than ordinary in this. [*To her*] Not fit to be told me, madam? You can have no interests wherein I am not concerned, and consequently the same reasons ought to be convincing to me, which create your satisfaction or disquiet. 45

LADY TOUCHWOOD

But those which cause my disquiet, I am willing to have remote from your hearing. Good my lord, don't press me.

LORD TOUCHWOOD

Don't oblige me to press you.

LADY TOUCHWOOD

Whatever it was, 'tis past; and that is better to be unknown which cannot be prevented; therefore let me beg you rest 50 satisfied—

LORD TOUCHWOOD

When you have told me, I will—

LADY TOUCHWOOD

You won't.

LORD TOUCHWOOD

By my life, my dear, I will.

LADY TOUCHWOOD

What if you can't? 55

LORD TOUCHWOOD

How? Then I must know, nay I will: no more trifling—I charge you tell me—by all our mutual peace to come; upon your duty—

LADY TOUCHWOOD

Nay, my lord, you need say no more, to make me lay my heart before you, but don't be thus transported; compose 60 yourself; it is not of concern to make you lose one minute's temper. 'Tis not indeed, my dear. Nay, by this kiss you shan't be angry. Oh Lord, I wish I had not told you

50 *rest* Q1 (to rest W1)

anything. Indeed, my lord, you have frighted me. Nay, look
pleased, I'll tell you.   65

LORD TOUCHWOOD
Well, well?

LADY TOUCHWOOD
Nay, but will you be calm?—Indeed it's nothing but—

LORD TOUCHWOOD
But what?

LADY TOUCHWOOD
But will you promise me not to be angry—nay you
must—not to be angry with Mellefont?—I dare swear he's   70
sorry—and were it to do again, would not—

LORD TOUCHWOOD
Sorry, for what? 'Death, you rack me with delay.

LADY TOUCHWOOD
Nay, no great matter, only—well I have your promise,—foh,
why nothing, only your nephew had a mind to amuse
himself sometimes with a little gallantry towards me. Nay, I   75
can't think he meant anything seriously, but methought it
looked oddly.

LORD TOUCHWOOD
Confusion and hell, what do I hear?

LADY TOUCHWOOD
Or maybe, he thought he was not enough akin to me, upon
your account, and had a mind to create a nearer relation on   80
his own; a lover you know, my lord—ha, ha, ha. Well but
that's all—now you have it; well, remember your promise,
my lord, and don't take any notice of it to him.

LORD TOUCHWOOD
No, no, no—damnation!

LADY TOUCHWOOD
Nay, I swear you must not—a little harmless mirth—only   85
misplaced, that's all—but if it were more, 'tis over now, and
all's well. For my part I have forgot it; and so has he, I
hope—for I have not heard anything from him these two
days.

LORD TOUCHWOOD
These two days! Is it so fresh? Unnatural villain! 'Death,   90
I'll have him stripped and turned naked out of my doors
this moment, and let him rot and perish, incestuous brute!

LADY TOUCHWOOD
Oh for heaven's sake, my lord, you'll ruin me if you take
such public notice of it, it will be a town-talk: consider your

---

90 *Death* abbreviated from 'God's death'; more commonly, "sdeath"

own and my honour—nay, I told you you would not be 95
satisfied when you knew it.

LORD TOUCHWOOD

Before I've done I will be satisfied. Ungrateful monster,
how long?—

LADY TOUCHWOOD

Lord, I don't know: I wish my lips had grown together
when I told you—almost a twelvemonth—nay, I won't tell 100
you any more, till you are yourself. Pray, my lord, don't let
the company see you in this disorder.—Yet, I confess, I
can't blame you; for I think I was never so surprised in my
life.—Who would have thought my nephew could have so
misconstrued my kindness?—But will you go into your 105
closet, and recover your temper? I'll make an excuse of
sudden business to the company, and come to you. Pray,
good dear my lord, let me beg you do now: I'll come
immediately, and tell you all; will you, my lord?

LORD TOUCHWOOD

I will—I am mute with wonder. 110

LADY TOUCHWOOD

Well but go now, here's somebody coming.

LORD TOUCHWOOD

Well I go—you won't stay, for I would hear more of this.

Exit LORD TOUCHWOOD

LADY TOUCHWOOD

I follow instantly.—So.

Enter MASKWELL

MASKWELL

This was a masterpiece, and did not need my help—though
I stood ready for a cue to come in and confirm all, had there 115
been occasion.

LADY TOUCHWOOD

Have you seen Mellefont?

MASKWELL

I have; and am to meet him here about this time.

LADY TOUCHWOOD

How does he bear his disappointment?

MASKWELL

Secure in my assistance, he seemed not much afflicted, but 120
rather laughed at the shallow artifice, which so little time
must of necessity discover. Yet he is apprehensive of some
farther design of yours, and has engaged me to watch you. I
believe he will hardly be able to prevent your plot, yet I

would have you use caution and expedition.   125

LADY TOUCHWOOD

Expedition indeed; for all we do must be performed in the
remaining part of this evening, and before the company
break up; lest my lord should cool, and have an opportunity
to talk with him privately—my lord must not see him again.

MASKWELL

By no means; therefore you must aggravate my lord's   130
displeasure to a degree that will admit of no conference with
him.—What think you of mentioning me?

LADY TOUCHWOOD

How?

MASKWELL

To my lord, as having been privy to Mellefont's design
upon you, but still using my utmost endeavours to dissuade   135
him; though my friendship and love to him has made me
conceal it; yet you may say, I threatened the next time he
attempted anything of that kind, to discover it to my lord.

LADY TOUCHWOOD

To what end is this?

MASKWELL

It will confirm my lord's opinion of my honour and   140
honesty, and create in him a new confidence in me, which
(should this design miscarry) will be necessary to the
forming another plot that I have in my head—(*aside*) to
cheat you, as well as the rest.

LADY TOUCHWOOD

I'll do it—I'll tell him you hindered him once from forcing   145
me.

MASKWELL

Excellent! Your ladyship has a most improving fancy. You
had best go to my lord, keep him as long as you can in his
closet, and I doubt not but you will mould him to what you
please; your guests are so engaged in their own follies and   150
intrigues, they'll miss neither of you.

LADY TOUCHWOOD

When shall we meet?—At eight this evening in my
chamber; there rejoice at our success, and toy away an hour
in mirth.

MASKWELL

I will not fail.   *Exit* LADY TOUCHWOOD   155

---

143 *forming* Q2 (forming of Q1)

143 *forming*. Q2's deletion of 'of' produces a slightly elliptical but elegant tightness.

I know what she means by toying away an hour well
enough. Pox I have lost all appetite to her; yet she's a fine
woman, I loved her once. But I don't know, since I have
been in a great measure kept by her, the case is altered;
what was my pleasure is become my duty: and I have as   160
little stomach to her now as if I were her husband. Should
she smoke my design upon Cynthia, I were in a fine pickle.
She has a damned penetrating head, and knows how to
interpret a coldness the right way; therefore I must
dissemble ardour and ecstacy, that's resolved: how easily   165
and pleasantly is that dissembled before fruition! Pox on't,
that a man can't drink without quenching his thirst. Ha!
Yonder comes Mellefont thoughtful. Let me think: meet
her at eight—hum—ha! By heaven I have it—if I can speak
to my lord before—was it my brain or Providence? No   170
matter which—I will deceive 'em all, and yet secure myself,
'twas a lucky thought! Well this double-dealing is a jewel.
Here he comes, now for me—

Enter MELLEFONT *musing;* MASKWELL *pretending not to see
him, walks by him, and speaks as it were to himself*

Mercy on us, what will the wickedness of this world come
to?   175

MELLEFONT

How now, Jack? What, so full of contemplation that you
run over!

MASKWELL

I'm glad you're come, for I could not contain myself any
longer: and was just going to give vent to a secret which
nobody but you ought to drink down.—Your aunt's just   180
gone from hence.

MELLEFONT

And having trusted thee with the secrets of her soul, thou
art villainously bent to discover 'em all to me, ha?

MASKWELL

I'm afraid my frailty leans that way—but I don't know

158 *I loved* Q1 (and I loved Q2)
172 *double-dealing is a jewel* reversal of proverb, 'plain-dealing is a jewel,'Tilley P382
173.1,2 S.D. so, Ed.(MASKWELL. . . himself.*precedes* Here Q1)

170 *was it my brain or Providence?* Aubrey Williams contends that Restoration
    playgoers were sufficiently conditioned through innumerable repetitions of the
    idea in sermons to be in no doubt of the true answer; e.g., Archbishop Tillotson;
    'what we think to be the effect of our own strength and resolution, of our own
    wisdom and contrivance, proceeds from a higher cause, which unseen to us,
    doth steer and govern us' (Williams, pp. 149-50).

whether I can in honour discover 'em all.   185

MELLEFONT

All, all, man; what, you may in honour betray her as far as
she betrays herself. No tragical design upon my person, I
hope.

MASKWELL

No, but it's a comical design upon mine.

MELLEFONT

What dost thou mean?   190

MASKWELL

Listen and be dumb, we have been bargaining about the
rate of your ruin—

MELLEFONT

Like any two guardians to an orphan heiress—well?

MASKWELL

And whereas pleasure is generally paid with mischief, what
mischief I do is to be paid with pleasure.   195

MELLEFONT

So when you've swallowed the potion, you sweeten your
mouth with a plum.

MASKWELL

You are merry, sir, but I shall probe your constitution. In
short, the price of your banishment is to be paid with the
person of—   200

MELLEFONT

Of Cynthia, and her fortune—why you forget you told me
this before.

MASKWELL

No, no—so far you are right; and I am, as an earnest of that
bargain, to have full and free possession of the person
of—your aunt.   205

MELLEFONT

Ha!—Foh, you trifle.

MASKWELL

By this light, I'm serious; all raillery apart—I knew 'twould
stun you: this evening at eight she will receive me in her
bedchamber.

MELLEFONT

Hell and the devil, is she abandoned of all grace?—Why the   210
woman is possessed—

185 *'em all* W1 (all Q1; them all W2)
195 *do* Q2 (shall do Q1)

---

185 *'em all.* W1's ''em' clarifies the sense.
195 *do.* Q2's 'do' implies future action with improved economy.

MASKWELL

Well, will you go in my stead?

MELLEFONT

By heaven into a hot furnace sooner.

MASKWELL

No, you would not—it would not be so convenient, as I can
order matters.   215

MELLEFONT

What d'ye mean?

MASKWELL

Mean? Not to disappoint the lady I assure you—ha, ha, ha,
how gravely he looks—come, come, I won't perplex you.
'Tis the only thing that Providence could have contrived to
make me capable of serving you, either to my inclination or   220
your own necessity.

MELLEFONT

How, how, for heaven's sake, dear Maskwell?

MASKWELL

Why thus—I'll go according to appointment; you shall have
notice at the critical minute to come and surprise your aunt
and me together: counterfeit a rage against me, and I'll   225
make my escape through the private passage from her
chamber, which I'll take care to leave open: 'twill be hard, if
then you can't bring her to any conditions. For this
discovery will disarm her of all defence, and leave her
entirely at your mercy: nay, she must ever after be in awe of 230
you.

MELLEFONT

Let me adore thee, my better genius! By heaven I think it is
not in the power of fate to disappoint my hopes—my hopes?
My certainty!

MASKWELL

Well, I'll meet you here, within a quarter of eight, and give   235
you notice.   *Exit*

MELLEFONT

Good fortune ever go along with thee.

Enter to him CARELESS

CARELESS

Mellefont, get out o'th' way, my Lady Plyant's coming, and
I shall never succeed while thou art in sight—though she

230 *awe* Q2 (one Q1)   236 *Exit* Q2 (*not in* Q1)

_____

230 *awe*. Q1's 'one' is clearly a compositor's misreading.

begins to tack about; but I made love a great while to no   240
purpose.

MELLEFONT

Why, what's the matter? She's convinced that I don't care
for her.

CARELESS

Pox I can't get an answer from her, that does not begin with
her honour, or her virtue, her religion, or some such cant.   245
Then she has told me the whole history of Sir Paul's nine
years' courtship: how he has lain for whole nights together
upon the stairs, before her chamber-door; and that the first
favour he received from her was a piece of an old scarlet
petticoat for a stomacher; which, since the day of his   250
marriage, he has, out of a piece of gallantry, converted into
a night-cap, and wears it still with much solemnity on his
anniversary wedding-night.

MELLEFONT

That I have seen, with the ceremony thereunto
belonging—for on that night he creeps in at the bed's feet   255
like a gulled bassa that has married a relation of the Grand
Signior's, and that night he has his arms at liberty. Did not
she tell you at what a distance she keeps him? He has
confessed to me that but at some certain times, that is I
suppose when she apprehends being with child, he never   260
has the privilege of using the familiarity of a husband with
his wife. He was once given to scrambling with his hands
and sprawling in his sleep; and ever since she has him
swaddled up in blankets, and his hands and feet swathed
down, and so put to bed; and there he lies with a great   265
beard, like a Russian bear upon a drift of snow. You are
very great with him, I wonder he never told you his
grievances, he will, I warrant you.

CARELESS

Excessively foolish!—But that which gives me most hopes
of her, is her telling me of the many temptations she has   270
resisted.

MELLEFONT

Nay, then you have her; for a woman's bragging to a man

244 *Pox* Q1 (*om.* W1)
250 *stomacher* waistcoat
256 *bassa* pasha, Turkish officer of high rank
257 *Signior's* Q1 (Signior W1)
262 *his* Q1 (a W1)

256-7 *a gulled. . .Signior's.* See Longer Notes, No. 3.

that she has overcome temptations is an argument that they
were weakly offered, and a challenge to him to engage her
more irresistibly. 'Tis only an enhancing the price of the 275
commodity, by telling you how many customers have
underbid her.

CARELESS

Nay, I don't despair—but still she has a grudging to you—I
talked to her t'other night at my Lord Froth's masquerade,
when I'm satisfied she knew me, and I had no reason to 280
complain of my reception; but I find women are not the
same barefaced and in masks,—and a visor disguises their
inclinations as much as their faces.

MELLEFONT

'Tis a mistake, for women may most properly be said to be
unmasked when they wear visors: for that secures them 285
from blushing, and being out of countenance, and next to
being in the dark, or alone, they are most truly themselves
in a visor mask. Here they come, I'll leave you. Ply her
close, and by and by clap a *billet-doux* into her hand; for a
woman never thinks a man truly in love with her, till he has 290
been fool enough to think of her out of her sight, and to lose
so much time as to write to her.   *Exit*

Enter SIR PAUL *and* LADY PLYANT

SIR PAUL

Shan't we disturb your meditation, Mr. Careless: you
would be private?

CARELESS

You bring that along with you, Sir Paul, that shall be 295
always welcome to my privacy.

SIR PAUL

Oh, sweet sir, you load your humble servants, both me and
my wife, with continual favours.

LADY PLYANT

Jesu, Sir Paul, what a phrase was there? You will be making
answers, and taking that upon you, which ought to lie upon 300
me: that you should have so little breeding to think Mr.
Careless did not apply himself to me! Pray what have you
about you to entertain anybody's privacy? I swear and
declare in the face of the world I'm ready to blush for your
ignorance.   305

278 *grudging* secret desire
282 *visor* mask that covered whole face
299 *Jesu* Q1 (*om.* Q2)
303 *about you* Q1 (*om.* W1)

SIR PAUL (*Aside to her*)

I acquiesce, my lady; but don't snub so loud.

LADY PLYANT

Mr. Careless, if a person that is wholly illiterate might be
supposed to be capable of being qualified to make a suitable
return to those obligations which you are pleased to confer
upon one that is wholly incapable of being qualified in all   310
those circumstances, I'm sure I should rather attempt it
than anything in the world; (*Curtsies*) for I'm sure there's
nothing in the world that I would rather. (*Curtsies*) But I
know Mr. Careless is so great a critic and so fine a
gentleman, that it is impossible for me—   315

CARELESS

Oh heavens! Madam, you confound me.

SIR PAUL

Gadsbud, she's a fine person—

LADY PLYANT

Oh Lord! Sir, pardon me, we women have not those
advantages: I know my own imperfections—but at the same
time you must give me leave to declare in the face of the   320
world that nobody is more sensible of favours and things;
for with the reserve of my honour, I assure you, Mr.
Careless, I don't know anything in the world I would refuse
to a person so meritorious—you'll pardon my want of
expression—   325

CARELESS

Oh your ladyship is abounding in all excellence,
particularly that of phrase.

LADY PLYANT

You are so obliging, sir.

CARELESS

Your ladyship is so charming.

SIR PAUL

So, now, now; now my lady.   330

LADY PLYANT

So well-bred.

CARELESS

So surprising.

LADY PLYANT

So well dressed, so *bonne mine*, so eloquent, so unaffected,

---

333 *bonne mine* W1 (boon mein Q1)

---

333 *bonne mine.* Appearance of good health, pleasant manner, etc. Congreve's latest
    intention may be respected here, as opposed to 'boon mein'; but Lady Plyant is
    quite likely to mispronounce French.

so easy, so free, so particular, so agreeable—

SIR PAUL

Ay, so, so, there.   335

CARELESS

Oh Lord, I beseech you, madam, don't—

LADY PLYANT

So gay, so graceful, so good teeth, so fine shape, so fine
limbs, so fine linen, and I don't doubt but you have a very
good skin, sir.

CARELESS

For heaven's sake, madam—I'm quite out of countenance.   340

SIR PAUL

And my lady's quite out of breath; or else you should
hear—gadsbud, you may talk of my Lady Froth!

CARELESS

Oh fie, fie, not to be named of a day—my Lady Froth is
very well in her accomplishments—but it is when my Lady
Plyant is not thought of—if that can ever be.   345

LADY PLYANT

Oh you overcome me—that is so excessive—

SIR PAUL

Nay, I swear and vow that was pretty.

CARELESS

Oh, Sir Paul, you are the happiest man alive. Such a lady,
that is the envy of her own sex, and the admiration of ours!

SIR PAUL

Your humble servant, I am, I thank heaven, in a fine way of   350
living, as I may say, peacefully and happily, and I think
need not envy any of my neighbours, blessed be
Providence—ay, truly, Mr. Careless, my lady is a great
blessing, a fine, discreet, well-spoken woman as you shall
see—if it becomes me to say so; and we live very   355
comfortably together; she is a little hasty sometimes, and so
am I; but mine's soon over, and then I'm so sorry—oh, Mr.
Careless, if it were not for one thing—

Enter BOY *with a letter, carries it to* SIR PAUL

LADY PLYANT

How often have you been told of that, you jackanapes?

SIR PAUL

Gadso, gadsbud—Tim, carry it to my lady, you should have   360

349 *own sex* W1 (sex Q1)

---

349 *own sex.* W1's 'own' takes the emphasis more satisfactorily than 'her', and
improves the speech-rhythm, for this character.

carried it to my lady first.

BOY

'Tis directed to your worship.

SIR PAUL

Well, well, my lady reads all letters first—child, do so no more; d'ye hear, Tim?

BOY

No, an please you.   365

Carries the letter to my lady and exit

SIR PAUL

A humour of my wife's, you know women have little fancies.—But as I was telling you, Mr. Careless, if it were not for one thing, I should think myself the happiest man in the world; indeed that touches me near, very near.

CARELESS

What can that be, Sir Paul?   370

SIR PAUL

Why, I have, I thank heaven, a very plentiful fortune, a good estate in the country, some houses in town, and some money, a pretty tolerable personal estate; and it is a great grief to me, indeed it is, Mr. Careless, that I have not a son to inherit this—'tis true, I have a daughter, and a fine   375 dutiful child she is, though I say it, blessed be Providence I may say; for indeed, Mr. Careless, I am mightily beholden to Providence—a poor unworthy sinner—but if I had a son, ah, that's my affliction, and my only affliction; indeed I cannot refrain tears when it comes in my mind.   *Cries*   380

CARELESS

Why, methinks that might be easily remedied—my lady's a fine, likely woman—

SIR PAUL

Oh, a fine, likely woman as you shall see in a summer's day—indeed she is, Mr. Careless, in all respects.

CARELESS

And I should not have taken you to have been so old—   385

SIR PAUL

Alas, that's not it, Mr. Careless. Ah! That's not it; no, no, you shoot wide of the mark a mile; indeed you do, that's not it, Mr. Careless; no, no, that's not it.

CARELESS

No? What can be the matter then?

---

365 *an* Q1 (and Q2; and't W2)
377 *beholden* W1 (beholding Q1)

SIR PAUL

You'll scarcely believe me, when I shall tell you—my lady is   390
so nice—it's very strange, but it's true: too true—she's so
very nice, that I don't believe she would touch a man for the
world—at least not above once a year; I'm sure I have found
it so; and alas, what's once a year to an old man, who would
do good in his generation? Indeed it's true, Mr. Careless, it   395
breaks my heart—I am her husband, as I may say, though
far unworthy of that honour, yet I am her husband; but
alas-a-day, I have no more familiarity with her person—as to
that matter—than with my own mother—no, indeed.

CARELESS

Alas-a-day, this is a lamentable story; my lady must be told   400
on't; she must i'faith, Sir Paul; 'tis an injury to the world.

SIR PAUL

Ah! Would to heaven you would, Mr. Careless; you are
mightily in her favour.

CARELESS

I warrant you, what, we must have a son some way or other.

SIR PAUL

Indeed, I should be mightily bound to you, if you could   405
bring it about, Mr. Careless.

LADY PLYANT

Here, Sir Paul, it's from your steward, here's a return of six
hundred pounds; you may take fifty of it for your next half
year.   *Gives him the letter*

Enter LORD FROTH, CYNTHIA

SIR PAUL

How does my girl? Come hither to thy father, poor lamb,   410
thou'rt melancholy.

LORD FROTH

Heaven, Sir Paul, you amaze me, of all things in the
world—you are never pleased but when we are all upon the
broad grin; all laugh and no company; ah, then 'tis such a
sight to see some teeth—sure you're a great admirer of my   415
Lady Whiffler, Mr. Sneer, and Sir Laurence Loud, and that
gang.

390 *my* Q2 (why my Q1)
408 *your next* Q1 (the next W1)
411 *melancholy* Q1 (melancholic W1)
416 *Whiffler* trifler, insignificant or contemptible person

390 *my.* Q1's 'why my' is verbose and uneuphonious.

SIR PAUL

    I vow and swear she's a very merry woman, but I think she
    laughs a little too much.

LORD FROTH

    Merry! Oh Lord, what a character that is of a woman of   420
    quality—you have been at my Lady Whiffler's upon her
    day, madam?

CYNTHIA

    Yes, my lord.—(*Aside*) I must humour this fool.

LORD FROTH

    Well and how? He! What is your sense of the conversation?

CYNTHIA

    Oh most ridiculous, a perpetual consort of laughing   425
    without any harmony; for sure, my lord, to laugh out of
    time is as disagreeable as to sing out of time or out of tune.

LORD FROTH

    He, he, he, right; and then, my Lady Whiffler is so
    ready—she always comes in three bars too soon—and then,
    what do they laugh at? For you know laughing without a   430
    jest is as impertinent, he, as, as—

CYNTHIA

    As dancing without a fiddle.

LORD FROTH

    Just, i'faith, that was at my tongue's end.

CYNTHIA

    But that cannot be properly said of them, for I think they
    are all in good nature with the world, and only laugh at one   435
    another; and you must allow they have all jests in their
    persons, though they have none in their conversation.

LORD FROTH

    True, as I'm a person of honour—for heaven's sake let us
    sacrifice 'em to mirth a little.

        Enter BOY *and whispers* [*to*] SIR PAUL

SIR PAUL

    Gads so.—Wife, wife, my Lady Plyant, I have a word.   440

LADY PLYANT

    I'm busy, Sir Paul, I wonder at your impertinence—

---

424 *conversation* W1 (conversation there Q1)

---

424 *conversation.* Q1's 'there' is superfluous, being understood; W1 suits Lord
    Froth's empty drawl.

431 *as, as.* . .Such failure to find a similitude was an established mark of a false wit
    (Lynch, p. 93).

CARELESS

[*Aside to* SIR PAUL] Sir Paul, hark'ee, I'm reasoning the
matter you know.—[*Aloud*] Madam,—if your ladyship
please, we'll discourse of this in the next room.

Exeunt CARELESS *and* LADY PLYANT

SIR PAUL

Oh ho, I wish you good success, I wish you good success.   445
Boy, tell my lady, when she has done, I would speak with
her below.   *Exit* SIR PAUL

Enter LADY FROTH *and* BRISK

LADY FROTH

Then you think that episode between Susan, the dairymaid,
and our coachman is not amiss? You know, I may suppose
the dairy in town, as well as in the country.   450

BRISK

Incomparable, let me perish—but then being an heroic
poem, had not you better call him a charioteer?
"Charioteer" sounds great; besides your ladyship's
coachman having a red face, and you comparing him to the
sun—and you know the sun is called "heaven's   455
charioteer."

LADY FROTH

Oh, infinitely better; I'm extremely beholden to you for the
hint; stay, we'll read over those half a score lines again.
(*Pulls out a paper*) Let me see here, you know what goes
before—the comparison, you know.   460
(*Reads*)   For as the sun shines every day,
                 So, of our coachman I may say—

BRISK

I'm afraid that simile won't do in wet weather—because you
say the sun shines every day.

LADY FROTH

No, for the sun it won't, but it will do for the coachman, for   465
you know there's most occasion for a coach in wet weather.

BRISK

Right, right, that saves all.

LADY FROTH

Then I don't say the sun shines all the day, but that he
peeps now and then; yet he does shine all the day too, you
know, though we don't see him.   470

457 *beholden* W1 (beholding Q1)

455-6 *heaven's charioteer.* Of a number of similar periphrases for the sun, derived
from Ovid's *currus diurnos,* listed by John Arthos, the nearest is Edward
Benlowes' 'circling charioteer of day', *Theophila* (1652), I, lxiii (*The Language of
Natural Description in Eighteenth-Century Poetry* [1966], pp. 386-8).

BRISK

Right, but the vulgar will never comprehend that.

LADY FROTH

Well, you shall hear—let me see.

(*Reads*)   For as the sun shines every day,
           So, of our coachman I may say,
           He shows his drunken fiery face,   475
           Just as the sun does, more or less.

BRISK

That's right, all's well, all's well. "More or less."

LADY FROTH (*Reads*)

      And when at night his labour's done,
      Then too, like heaven's charioteer, the sun—

Ay, "charioteer" does better.   480

      Into the dairy he descends,
      And there his whipping and his driving ends;
      There he's secure from danger of a bilk,
      His fare is paid him, and he sets in milk.

For Susan, you know, is Thetis, and so—   485

BRISK

Incomparable well and proper, egad—but I have one exception to make—don't you think "bilk" (I know it's good rhyme), but don't you think "bilk" and "fare" too like a hackney-coachman?

LADY FROTH

I swear and vow I'm afraid so.—And yet our Jehu was a   490 hackney-coachman, when my lord took him.

BRISK

Was he? I'm answered, if Jehu was a hackney-coachman.—You may put that in the marginal notes

---

477 *"More or less"* W1 (*not in* Q1)
483 *bilk* having someone go off without paying the fare; a deception
484 *sets in* sits to partake of a meal, begins (also of sun)
490 *Jehu* prince said to drive his chariot furiously, 2 Kings, 9:20
492 *Was he* W1 (Was that he then Q1)
493 *in* Q2 (into Q1)

---

477 *"More or less"*. The echo stresses their shared fatuity: a definite improvement.
485 *Thetis*. A sea-dwelling Nereid, mother of Achilles, who provided succour to both Hephaestus and Dionysus when they took refuge in the sea; and so, she might give sustenance to the coachman, as an Apollo-figure.
492-4 *Was. . .criticism*. The Q2 and W1 variants tighten the style.
493 *marginal notes*. Cf. Dryden, 'I have avoided as much as I cou'd possibly the borrow'd Learning of Marginal Notes and Illustrations' ('Argument of the first Satyr' of Juvenal [1693], *Works*, IV, 92).

though, to prevent criticism—only mark it with a small
asterism, and say, "Jehu was formerly a hackney- 495
coachman."

LADY FROTH

I will; you'd oblige me extremely to write notes to the
whole poem.

BRISK

With all my heart and soul, and proud of the vast honour,
let me perish. 500

LORD FROTH

He, he, he, my dear, have you done?—Won't you join with
us, we were laughing at my Lady Whiffler, and Mr. Sneer?

LADY FROTH

—Ay my dear—were you? Oh filthy Mr. Sneer; he's a
nauseous figure, a most fulsamic fop, foh—he spent two
days together in going about Covent Garden to suit the 505
lining of his coach with his complexion.

LORD FROTH

Oh silly! Yet his aunt is as fond of him, as if she had
brought the ape into the world herself.

BRISK

Who, my Lady Toothless? Oh, she's a mortifying spectacle;
she's always chewing the cud like an old ewe. 510

CYNTHIA

Fie, Mr. Brisk, 'tis eringos for her cough.

LADY FROTH

I have seen her take 'em half chewed out of her mouth, to
laugh, and then put 'em in again—foh!

LORD FROTH

Foh!

LADY FROTH

Then she's always ready to laugh when Sneer offers to 515
speak—and sits in expectation of his no jest, with her gums
bare, and her mouth open.—

BRISK

Like an oyster at low ebb, egad—ha, ha, ha.

494 *criticism* Q2 (criticisms Q1)   495 *asterism* group of three asterisks
504 *fulsamic* fulsome: wearisome, offensive to good taste
511 *'tis eringos* Q1 (eringos W1), 'the candied root of the Sea Holly (*Eryngium
maritimum*), formerly used as a sweetmeat, and regarded as an aphrodisiac'
(Summers)

518 *Like. . .ebb.* He echoes a phrase from Suckling's *The Goblins* (published 1646),
III,ii.40 *(The Works of Sir John Suckling,* 2 vols., *The Plays,* ed. L.A. Beaurline
[Oxford, 1971], p. 143), cf. Lynch, pp. 92-3.

CYNTHIA (*Aside*)

Well, I find there are no fools so inconsiderable in themselves, but they can render other people contemptible 520 by exposing their infirmities.

LADY FROTH

Then that t'other great strapping lady—I can't hit of her name; the old fat fool that paints so exorbitantly.

BRISK

I know whom you mean—but deuce take me, I can't hit of her name neither.—Paints d'ye say? Why she lays it on with 525 a trowel—then she has a great beard that bristles through it, and makes her look as if she were plastered with lime and hair, let me perish.

LADY FROTH

Oh you made a song upon her, Mr. Brisk.

BRISK

He? Egad, so I did—my lord can sing it. 530

CYNTHIA

Oh good my lord let's hear it.

BRISK

'Tis not a song neither—it's a sort of an epigram, or rather an epigrammatic sonnet; I don't know what to call it, but it's satire.—Sing it, my lord.

SONG

LORD FROTH (*Sings*)

Ancient Phillis has young graces, 535
'Tis a strange thing, but a true one;
Shall I tell you how?
She herself makes her own faces,
And each morning wears a new one;
Where's the wonder now? 540

BRISK

Short, but there's salt in't; my way of writing, egad.

Enter FOOTMAN

LADY FROTH

How now?

FOOTMAN

Your ladyship's chair is come.

---

521 *by* W1 (in Q1)
525 *d'ye* Q2 (d'ee Q1)

---

521 *by*. W1 clarifies the sense, and avoids repetition of the syllable 'in.'

LADY FROTH

Is nurse and the child in it?

FOOTMAN

Yes, madam.   [*Exit*]   545

LADY FROTH

Oh the dear creature! Let's go see it.

LORD FROTH

I swear, my dear, you'll spoil that child, with sending it to
and again so often, this is the seventh time the chair has
gone for her today.

LADY FROTH

Oh law, I swear it's but the sixth,—and I ha'n't seen her   550
these two hours—the poor dear creature—I swear, my lord,
you don't love poor little Sappho—come, my dear Cynthia,
Mr. Brisk, we'll go see Sappho, though my lord won't.

CYNTHIA

I'll wait upon your ladyship.

BRISK

Pray, madam, how old is Lady Sappho.   555

LADY FROTH

Three quarters, but I swear she has a world of wit, and can
sing a tune already. My lord, won't you go? Won't you?
What, not to see Sapph? Pray, my lord, come see little
Sapph. I knew you could not stay. *Exeunt* [*all but* CYNTHIA]

CYNTHIA

'Tis not so hard to counterfeit joy in the depth of affliction,   560
as to dissemble mirth in company of fools.—Why should I
call 'em fools? The world thinks better of 'em; for these
have quality and education, wit and fine conversation, are
received and admired by the world—if not, they like and
admire themselves—and why is not that true wisdom, for   565
'tis happiness? And for aught I know, we have misapplied
the name all this while, and mistaken the thing: since
          If happiness in self-content is placed,
          The wise are wretched, and fools only blessed. *Exit*

---

552 *Sappho.* The archetypal poetess; cf. 'such Sappho's of our Age, as I see here,'
    Thomas Wright, *The Female Virtuosos* (1693), II,i (p.16).
561-9 Cf. Ecclesiastes, 7:4; Erasmus, *The Praise of Folly* (1514): 'For what is so
    foolish as to be pleased with yourself? Or to admire yourself?. . .[Yet] since
    happiness, for the most part, is to wish to be what you are, . . .[self-love] brings
    it about in a short time,' whereas the wise are gloomy (*The Essential Erasmus*,
    transl. and ed. J.D. Dolan [New York, 1964], p. 114).

Act IV, Scene i

[*The Gallery*]
Enter MELLEFONT *and* CYNTHIA

CYNTHIA
    I heard him loud as I came by the closet-door, and my lady
    with him, but she seemed to moderate his passion.
MELLEFONT
    Ay, hell thank her, as gentle breezes moderate a fire; but I
    shall counter-work her spells, and ride the witch in her own
    bridle.   5
CYNTHIA
    It's impossible; she'll cast beyond you still—I'll lay my life
    it will never be a match.
MELLEFONT
    What!
CYNTHIA
    Between you and me.
MELLEFONT
    Why so?   10
CYNTHIA
    My mind gives me it won't—because we are both willing;
    we each of us strive to reach the goal, and hinder one
    another in the race; I swear it never does well when the
    parties are so agreed—for when people walk hand in hand,
    there's neither overtaking nor meeting: we hunt in couples   15
    where we both pursue the same game, but forget one
    another; and 'tis because we are so near that we don't think
    of coming together.
MELLEFONT
    Hum, 'gad I believe there's something in't;—marriage is the
    game that we hunt, and while we think that we only have it   20
    in view, I don't see but we have it in our power.

6 *cast* contrive
11 *willing* Q2 (so willing Q1)

4-5 *ride. . .bridle.* 'In allusion to the popular belief that a witch by casting a bridle
    over a man's head could enchant him, and compel him to carry her as a horse'
    (Summers). In Shadwell's *The Lancashire Witches* (1682), revived in 1691, Mal
    Spencer used Clod in this fashion.
11 *willing.* Q2's deletion of 'so' avoids repetition of the word in two different
    senses.

CYNTHIA

Within reach; for example, give me your hand; you have
looked through the wrong end of the perspective all this
while; for nothing has been between us but our fears.

MELLEFONT

I don't know why we should not steal out of the house this   25
very moment and marry one another, without consideration
or the fear of repentance. Pox o' fortune, portion,
settlements and jointures.

CYNTHIA

Ay, ay, what have we to do with 'em? You know we marry
for love.   30

MELLEFONT

Love, love, downright very villainous love.

CYNTHIA

And he that can't live upon love deserves to die in a
ditch.—Here then, I give you my promise, in spite of duty,
any temptation of wealth, your inconstancy, or my own
inclination to change—   35

MELLEFONT

To run most wilfully and unreasonably away with me this
moment, and be married.

CYNTHIA

Hold—never to marry anybody else.

MELLEFONT

That's but a kind of negative consent.—Why, you won't
baulk the frolic?   40

CYNTHIA

If you had not been so assured of your own conduct I would
not—but 'tis reasonable that since I consent to like a man
without the vile consideration of money, he should give me
a very evident demonstration of his wit; therefore let me see
you undermine my Lady Touchwood, as you boasted, and   45
force her to give her consent, and then—

22 *you have* W1 (why have you Q1)
26 *very moment* W1 (moment Q1)

22 *you have.* W1 offers a clearer line of thought, and greater elegance.
22-3 *you. . .perspective.* A perspective being a spy-glass or telescope, the expression
    is oddly used; it normally meant to see something as smaller than it really is,
    rather than larger.
26 *very moment.* W1's 'very' adds strength.
34-5 *my. . .change.* (a) Proverbial, 'A woman is ever mutable,' Tilley W674; (b) like
    her namesake the moon.

MELLEFONT

I'll do't.

CYNTIIIA

And I'll do't.

MELLEFONT

This very next ensuing hour of eight o'clock is the last
minute of her reign, unless the devil assist her *in propria*   50
persona.

CYNTHIA

Well, if the devil should assist her, and your plot
miscarry;—

MELLEFONT

Ay, what am I to trust to then?

CYNTHIA

Why if you give me very clear demonstration that it was the   55
devil, I'll allow for irresistible odds. But if I find it to be
only chance, or destiny, or unlucky stars, or anything but
the very devil, I'm inexorable: only still I'll keep my word,
and live a maid for your sake.

MELLEFONT

And you won't die one, for your own, so still there's hope.   60

CYNTHIA

Here's my mother-in-law and your friend Careless; I would
not have 'em see us together yet.   *Exeunt*

[Act IV, Scene ii]

Enter CARELESS *and* LADY PLYANT

LADY PLYANT

I swear, Mr. Careless, you are very alluring—and say so
many fine things, and nothing is so moving to me as a fine
thing. Well, I must do you this justice, and declare in the
face of the world, never anybody gained so far upon me as
yourself; with blushes I must own it, you have shaken, as I   5
may say, the very foundation of my honour.—Well, sure if I
escape your importunities, I shall value myself as long as I
live, I swear.

CARELESS (*Sighing*)

And despise me.

LADY PLYANT

The last of any man in the world, by my purity; now you   10
make me swear.—Oh gratitude forbid, that I should ever be

50-1 *in propria persona* in his own person

wanting in a respectful acknowledgment of an entire
resignation of all my best wishes, for the person and parts of
so accomplished a person, whose merit challenges much
more, I'm sure, than my illiterate praises can description—   15

CARELESS (*In a whining tone*)

Ah heavens, madam, you ruin me with kindness; your
charming tongue pursues the victory of your eyes, while at
your feet your poor adorer dies.   [*Kneels*]

LADY PLYANT

Ah! very fine.

CARELESS (*Still whining*)

Ah why are you so fair, so bewitching fair? Oh let me grow   20
to the ground here, and feast upon that hand; oh let me
press it to my heart, my trembling heart, the nimble
movement shall instruct your pulse, and teach it to alarm
desire. (*Aside*) Zoons I'm almost at the end of my cant, if
she does not yield quickly.   25

LADY PLYANT

Oh that's so passionate and fine, I cannot hear it—I am not
safe if I stay, and must leave you.

CARELESS

And must you leave me! Rather let me languish out a
wretched life, and breathe my soul beneath your feet.
(*Aside*) I must say the same thing over again, and can't help   30
it.

LADY PLYANT

I swear I am ready to languish too—oh my honour! Whither
is it going? I protest you have given me the palpitation of
the heart.

CARELESS

Can you be so cruel?—   35

LADY PLYANT

Oh rise I beseech you, say no more till you rise.—Why did
you kneel so long? I swear I was so transported, I did not see
it.—Well, to show you how far you have gained upon me; I
assure you if Sir Paul should die, of all mankind there's
none I'd sooner make my second choice.   40

CARELESS [*Rising*]

Oh heaven! I can't outlive this night without your

22 *trembling* Q2 (aching trembling Q1)

16-18 *your. . .dies.* Ewald prints as a verse couplet. Where Careless kneels, and later
rises, is not clear.
22 *trembling.* Q1's 'aching' is awkward, and disrupts the thought.

favour—I feel my spirits faint, a general dampness
overspreads my face, a cold, deadly dew already vents
through all my pores, and will tomorrow wash me forever
from your sight, and drown me in my tomb.   45

LADY PLYANT

Oh you have conquered, sweet, melting, moving sir, you
have conquered—what heart of marble can refrain to weep,
and yield to such sad sayings?—   *Cries*

CARELESS

I thank heaven, they are the saddest that I ever said.—Oh!
(*Aside*) I shall never contain laughter.   50

LADY PLYANT

Oh, I yield myself all up to your uncontrollable
embraces—say, thou dear, dying man, when, where, and
how?—Ah, there's Sir Paul.

Enter SIR PAUL *and* CYNTHIA

CARELESS

'Slife yonder's Sir Paul, but if he were not come, I'm so
transported I cannot speak.—(*Gives her a note*) This note   55
will inform you.   *Exit*

SIR PAUL

Thou art my tender lambkin, and shalt do what thou
wilt—but endeavour to forget this Mellefont.

CYNTHIA

I would obey you to my power, sir; but if I have not him, I
have sworn never to marry.   60

SIR PAUL

Never to marry! Heaven forbid; must I neither have sons
nor grandsons? Must the family of the Plyants be utterly
extinct for want of issue male? Oh impiety! But did you
swear, did that sweet creature swear? Ha? How durst you

---

61 *Heaven* Q1 (Heavens Q2)

43 *a cold, deadly dew.* Cf. the dying Alexander, 'What means this deadly dew upon
   my forehead?' (*The Rival Queens*, V,i. 239); also, the 'cold and deadly draught'
   of poison in Lee's *Theodosius* (1680), V,iv. 52.
63-4 *But. . .Ha.* Cf. Alexander, 'Ha! did she swear? did that sweet Creature swear?'
   (*The Rival Queens*, II,i. 350).
64-76 *How. . .break it.* Cynthia is in the position of those Non-jurors who refused
   to take the oaths of supremacy and allegiance to William and Mary, on the
   ground that they remained bound to their oaths previously sworn to James II.
   Much ingenuity was currently being devoted to trying to persuade them that
   their prior oaths were 'of none effect' (see J.P. Kenyon, *Revolution Principles*
   [Cambridge, 1977], pp. 21-31).

swear without my consent, ha? Gadsbud, who am I?   65

CYNTHIA

Pray don't be angry, sir; when I swore, I had your consent;
and therefore I swore.

SIR PAUL

Why then the revoking my consent does annul, or make of
none effect your oath; so you may unswear it again—the law
will allow it.   70

CYNTHIA

Ay, but my conscience never will.

SIR PAUL

Gadsbud no matter for that, conscience and law never go
together; you must not expect that.

LADY PLYANT

Ay, but Sir Paul, I conceive if she has swore, d'ye mark me,
if she has once sworn: it is most unchristian, inhuman, and   75
obscene that she should break it.—(*Aside*) I'll make up the
match again, because Mr. Careless said it would oblige him.

SIR PAUL

Does your ladyship conceive so?—Why I was of that
opinion once too—nay if your ladyship conceives so, I'm of
that opinion again; but I can neither find my lord nor my   80
lady to know what they intend.

LADY PLYANT

I'm satisfied that my cousin Mellefont has been much
wronged.

CYNTHIA (*Aside*)

I'm amazed to find her of our side, for I'm sure she loved
him.   85

LADY PLYANT

I know my Lady Touchwood has no kindness for him; and
besides, I have been informed by Mr. Careless, that
Mellefont had never anything more than a profound
respect—that he has owned himself to be my admirer 'tis
true, but he was never so presumptuous to entertain any   90
dishonourable notions of things; so that if this be made
plain—I don't see how my daughter can in conscience, or
honour, or anything in the world—

65 *ha* Q1 (ah W1)   76 *the* W1 (this Q1)
75 *inhuman* Q2 (inhumane Q1)   90 *was never* Q2 (never was Q1)

---

76 *the.* W1's less obtrusive 'the' is preferable to 'this,' there being no question as to
which match is meant.

90 *was never.* W1's word-order gives the better rhythm and placing of stress.

SIR PAUL

Indeed if this be made plain, as my lady your mother says, child—   95

LADY PLYANT

Plain! I was informed of it by Mr. Careless—and I assure you Mr. Careless is a person—that has a most extraordinary respect and honour for you, Sir Paul.

CYNTHIA (*Aside*)

And for your ladyship too, I believe, or else you had not changed sides so soon; now I begin to find it.   100

SIR PAUL

I am much obliged to Mr. Careless really, he is a person that I have a great value for, not only for that, but because he has a great veneration for your ladyship.

LADY PLYANT

Oh 'las, no indeed, Sir Paul, 'tis upon your account.

SIR PAUL

No, I protest and vow, I have no title to his esteem, but in   105
having the honour to appertain in some measure to your ladyship, that's all.

LADY PLYANT

Oh law now, I swear and declare, it shan't be so, you're too modest, Sir Paul.

SIR PAUL

It becomes me, when there is any comparison made,   110
between—

LADY PLYANT

Oh fie, fie, Sir Paul, you'll put me out of countenance—your very obedient and affectionate wife; that's all—and highly honoured in that title.

SIR PAUL

Gadsbud, I am transported! Give me leave to kiss your   115
ladyship's hand.

CYNTHIA (*Aside*)

That my poor father should be so very silly!

LADY PLYANT

My lip indeed, Sir Paul, I swear you shall.

He kisses her, and bows very low

SIR PAUL

I humbly thank your ladyship.—[*Aside*] I don't know whether I fly on ground, or walk in air—gadsbud, she was   120
never thus before—well, I must own myself the most beholden to Mr. Careless—as sure as can be this is all his

doing—something that he has said; well, 'tis a rare thing to
have an ingenious friend. [*To her*] Well, your ladyship is of
opinion that the match may go forward?   125

LADY PLYANT

By all means—Mr. Careless has satisfied me of the matter.

SIR PAUL

Well, why then lamb, you may keep your oath, but have a
care of making rash vows; come hither to me, and kiss Papa.

LADY PLYANT [*Aside*]

I swear and declare, I am in such a twitter to read Mr.
Careless his letter, that I can't forbear any longer—but   130
though I may read all letters first by prerogative, yet I'll be
sure to be unsuspected this time.—[*To him*] Sir Paul.

SIR PAUL

Did your ladyship call?

LADY PLYANT

Nay, not to interrupt you my dear—only lend me your
letter, which you had from your steward today: I would   135
look upon the account again; and maybe increase your
allowance.

SIR PAUL

There it is, madam; do you want a pen and ink?
                                        Bows and gives the letter

LADY PLYANT

No, no, nothing else, I thank you, Sir Paul.—(*Aside*) So now
I can read my own letter under the cover of his.   140

SIR PAUL [*To* CYNTHIA]

He? And wilt thou bring a grandson at nine months'
end—he? A brave, chopping boy.—I'll settle a thousand
pound a year upon the rogue as soon as ever he looks me in
the face, I will gadsbud. I'm overjoyed to think I have any
of my family that will bring children into the world. For I   145
would fain have some resemblance of myself in my
posterity, he, Thy? Can't you contrive that affair, girl? Do
gadsbud, think on thy old father; heh? Make the young
rogue as like as you can.

CYNTHIA

I'm glad to see you so merry, sir.   150

SIR PAUL

Merry, gadsbud I'm serious, I'll give thee five hundred

---

123 *doing*. Q2's singular form fits the context and the verb.
129 *am in such*. Q1's omission of 'in' was probably a mistake.

pound for every inch of him that resembles me; ah this eye,
this left eye! A thousand pound for this left eye. This has
done execution in its time, girl; why, thou hast my leer,
hussy, just thy father's leer.—Let it be transmitted to the   155
young rogue by the help of imagination; why, 'tis the mark
of our family, Thy; our house is distinguished by a
languishing eye, as the House of Austria is by a thick
lip.—Ah! When I was of your age, hussy, I would have held
fifty to one, I could have drawn my own picture—gadsbud I   160
could have done—not so much as you neither,—but—nay,
don't blush—

CYNTHIA

I don't blush sir, for I vow I don't understand—

SIR PAUL

Pshaw, pshaw, you fib you baggage, you do understand,
and you shall understand; come don't be so nice, gadsbud   165
don't learn after your mother-in-law my lady here: marry,
heaven forbid that you should follow her example, that
would spoil all indeed. Bless us, if you should take a vagary
and make a rash resolution on your wedding night to die a
maid, as she did; all were ruined, all my hopes lost—my   170
heart would break, and my estate would be left to the wide
world, he? I hope you are a better Christian than to think of
living a nun; he? Answer me.

CYNTHIA

I'm all obedience, sir, to your commands.

LADY PLYANT (*Having read the letter*)

Oh, dear Mr. Careless, I swear he writes charmingly, and   175
he looks charmingly, and he has charmed me, as much as I
have charmed him; and so I'll tell him in the wardrobe
when 'tis dark. Oh crimine! I hope Sir Paul has not seen

153 *thousand pound* Q2 (1000*l.* Q1)
154 *leer* face; appearance
173 *living* Q2 (being Q1)
175 *writes charmingly* W1 (writes charmingly, and he talks charmingly Q1)
178 *crimine* variant of 'Gemini'

152-4 *ah. . .time.* He echoes Sir Thomas Reveller, 'ah that Eye, Sir *Thomas,* the
Leer of the left Eye has broken many a heart, you old Rogue,' in William
Mountfort, *Greenwich Park* (1691) I,iii (p. 5).

158-9 *as. . .lip.* The Habsburg princes 'were noted for. . .a heavy, protruding
underjaw and thick, hanging lip' (Summers).

173 *living.* Q2's reading here conveys the intended sense ('preserving a state of nun-
like chastity') more precisely than 'being.'

175 *writes charmingly.* W1's deletion of some words achieves economy with no real
loss of effect.

both letters.

(*Puts the wrong letter hastily up, and gives him her own*)
[*To him*] Sir Paul, here's your letter, tomorrow morning I'll   180
settle accounts to your advantage.

Enter BRISK

BRISK

Sir Paul, gadsbud you're an uncivil person, let me tell you,
and all that; and I did not think it had been in you.

SIR PAUL

Oh law, what's the matter now? I hope you are not angry,
Mr. Brisk.   185

BRISK

Deuce take me I believe you intend to marry your daughter
yourself; you're always brooding over her like an old hen, as
if she were not well hatched, egad, he?

SIR PAUL

Good strange! Mr. Brisk is such a merry, facetious person,
he, he, he. No, no, I have done with her, I have done with   190
her now.

BRISK

The fiddles have stayed this hour in the hall, and my Lord
Froth wants a partner, we can never begin without her.

SIR PAUL

Go, go, child, go, get you gone and dance and be merry, I'll
come and look at you by and by.—Where's my son   195
Mellefont?   *Exit* CYNTHIA

LADY PLYANT

I'll send him to them, I know where he is.—   *Exit*

BRISK

Sir Paul, will you send Careless into the hall if you meet
him?

SIR PAUL

I will, I will, I'll go and look for him on purpose.   *Exit* 200

BRISK

So now they are all gone, and I have an opportunity to
practise.—Ah! My dear Lady Froth! She's a most engaging
creature, if she were not so fond of that damned coxcombly
lord of hers; and yet I am forced to allow him wit too, to

178.1 *wrong* Q1 (*om.* W2)
181 *accounts* W1 (the accounts Q1)
192 *fiddles* Q1, W1 (fiddlers Q2)

---

181 *accounts*. W1's deletion again tightens the style.

keep in with him.—No matter, she's a woman of parts, and   205
egad parts will carry her. She said she would follow me into
the gallery,—now to make my approaches—hem, hem!
Ah ma-(*bows*)-dam!—Pox on't, why should I disparage my
parts by thinking what to say? None but dull rogues *think*;
witty men, like rich fellows, are always ready for all   210
expenses; while your blockheads, like poor needy
scoundrels, are forced to examine their stock, and forecast
the charges of the day. Here she comes, I'll seem not to see
her, and try to win her with a new airy invention of my
own, hem!   215

Enter LADY FROTH

BRISK (*Sings, walking about*)
"I'm sick with love," ha, ha, ha, "prithee come cure me.
I'm sick with," *&c.*
Oh ye powers! Oh my Lady Froth, my Lady Froth! My
Lady Froth! Heigho! Break heart! Gods, I thank you.
Stands musing with his arms across

LADY FROTH
Oh heavens Mr. Brisk! What's the matter?   220

BRISK
My Lady Froth! Your ladyship's most humble
servant;—the matter, madam? Nothing, madam, nothing at
all egad. I was fallen into the most agreeable amusement in
the whole province of contemplation: that's all.—(*Aside*) I'll
seem to conceal my passion, and that will look like respect.   225

LADY FROTH
Bless me, why did you call out upon me so loud?—

BRISK
Oh Lord, I, madam! I beseech your ladyship—when?

LADY FROTH
Just now as I came in; bless me, why, don't you know it?

BRISK
Not I, let me perish—but did I? Strange! I confess your
ladyship was in my thoughts; and I was in a sort of dream   230
that did in a manner represent a very pleasing object to my
imagination, but—but did I indeed?—To see how love and
murder will out. But did I really name my Lady Froth?

LADY FROTH
Three times aloud, as I love letters—but did you talk of
love? Oh Parnassus! Who would have thought Mr. Brisk   235

232-3 *how...out.* Proverbial, Tilley L520, M1315; cf. *Twelfth Night*, III,i. 159-60.

could have been in love, ha, ha, ha? Oh heavens, I thought
you could have no mistress but the nine Muses.

BRISK

No more I have egad, for I adore 'em all in your
ladyship—let me perish, I don't know whether to be
splenetic or airy upon't; the deuce take me if I can tell   240
whether I am glad or sorry that your ladyship has made the
discovery.

LADY FROTH

Oh be merry by all means—Prince Volscius in love! Ha, ha,
ha.

BRISK

Oh barbarous, to turn me into ridicule! Yet, ha, ha, ha. The   245
deuce take me, I can't help laughing myself, ha, ha, ha; yet
by heavens I have a violent passion for your ladyship,
seriously.

LADY FROTH

Seriously? Ha, ha, ha.

BRISK

Seriously, ha, ha, ha. Gad I have, for all I laugh.   250

LADY FROTH

Ha, ha, ha! What d'ye think I laugh at? Ha, ha, ha.

BRISK

Me egad, ha, ha.

LADY FROTH

No, the deuce take me if I don't laugh at myself; for hang
me if I have not a violent passion for Mr. Brisk, ha, ha, ha.

BRISK

Seriously?   255

LADY FROTH

Seriously, ha, ha, ha.

BRISK

That's well enough; let me perish, ha, ha, ha. Oh
miraculous, what a happy discovery. Ah my dear charming
Lady Froth!

---

246 *myself* Q2 (myself neither Q1)
247 *a violent* Q2 (violent Q1)

---

243 *Volscius.* In Buckingham's *The Rehearsal* (1671), III,v, Amarillis and Chloris
     exclaim 'How! Prince *Volscius* in love? Ha, ha, ha,' and go out 'laughing.' He
     has been suddenly stricken with love, and hence with paralysing indecision
     between the demands of love and honour.
246 *myself.* Q2's omission of 'neither' tightens the rhythm.
247 *a violent.* Q1's omission of the article is a corruption.

LADY FROTH
   Oh my adored Mr. Brisk!   *Embrace* 260

              Enter LORD FROTH

LORD FROTH
   The company are all ready—How now!
BRISK (*Softly to her*)
   Zoons, madam, there's my lord.
LADY FROTH
   [*Softly to him*] Take no notice—but observe me—[*Aloud*]
   Now cast off, and meet me at the lower end of the room,
   and then join hands again; I could teach my lord this dance 265
   purely, but I vow, Mr. Brisk, I can't tell how to come so
   near any other man. (*They pretend to practise part of a
   country-dance*) Oh here's my lord, now you shall see me do
   it with him.
LORD FROTH (*Aside*)
   Oh I see there's no harm yet—but I don't like this 270
   familiarity.
LADY FROTH
   Shall you and I do our close dance, to show Mr. Brisk?
LORD FROTH
   No, my dear, do it with him.
LADY FROTH
   I'll do it with him, my lord, when you are out of the way.
BRISK (*Aside*)
   That's good egad, that's good, deuce take me I can hardly 275
   hold laughing in his face.
LORD FROTH
   Any other time, my dear, or we'll dance it below.
LADY FROTH
   With all my heart.
BRISK
   Come my lord, I'll wait on you.—(*To her*) My charming 280
   witty angel!
LADY FROTH
   We shall have whispering time enough, you know, since we
   are partners.   *Exeunt*

[Act IV, Scene iii]

           Enter LADY PLYANT *and* CARELESS

LADY PLYANT
   Oh Mr. Careless, Mr. Careless, I'm ruined, I'm undone!

CARELESS

What's the matter, madam?

LADY PLYANT

Oh the unluckiest accident, I'm afraid I shan't live to tell it
you.

CARELESS

Heaven forbid! What is it?   5

LADY PLYANT

I'm in such a fright; the strangest quandary and *præmunire*!
I'm all over in a universal agitation, I dare swear every
circumstance of me trembles.—Oh your letter, your letter!
By an unfortunate mistake, I have given Sir Paul your letter
instead of his own.   10

CARELESS

That was unlucky.

LADY PLYANT

Oh yonder he comes reading of it, for heaven's sake step in
here and advise me quickly, before he sees.   *Exeunt*

[Act IV, Scene iv]

Enter SIR PAUL *with the letter*

SIR PAUL

—Oh Providence, what a conspiracy have I discovered—but
let me see to make an end on't.—(*Reads*) Hum—"After
supper in the wardrobe by the gallery. If Sir Paul should
surprise us, I have a commission from him to treat with you
about the very matter of fact."—Matter of fact! Very pretty;   5
it seems then I am conducing to my own cuckoldom; why
this is the very traitorous position of taking up arms by my
authority, against my person! Well, let me see—"Till then I
languish in expectation of my adored charmer.
                                Dying Ned Careless."   10
Gadsbud, would that were matter of fact too. Die and be
damned for a Judas Maccabeus, and Iscariot both. Oh
friendship! What art thou but a name! Henceforward let no

6 *præmunire*. Great trouble, comparable to the punishments inflicted for actions
in contempt of the royal prerogative.

6-8 *why. . .person.* Such had been the position of Parliament in 1642; cf. the
preamble to the Excise Ordinance.

12 *Judas Maccabeus.* A Jewish military hero of extreme boldness (died 160 B.C.), see
I Maccabees, 3-9.

man make a friend that would not be a cuckold: for
whomsoever he receives into his bosom, will find the way to   15
his bed, and there return his caresses with interest to his
wife. Have I for this been pinioned night after night for
three years past? Have I been swathed in blankets till I have
been even deprived of motion, and rendered uncapable of
using the common benefits of nature? Have I approached   20
the marriage bed with reverence as to a sacred shrine, and
denied myself the enjoyment of lawful domestic pleasures
to preserve its purity, and must I now find it polluted by
foreign iniquity? Oh my Lady Plyant, you were chaste as
ice, but you are melted now, and false as water.—But   25
Providence has been constant to me in discovering this
conspiracy; still I am beholden to Providence, if it were not
for Providence, sure poor Sir Paul thy heart would break.

Enter LADY PLYANT

LADY PLYANT
So, sir, I see you have read the letter;—well now, Sir Paul,
what do you think of your friend Careless? Has he been   30
treacherous, or did you give his insolence a license to make
trial of your wife's suspected virtue? (*Snatches the letter as in
anger*) D'ye see here? Look, read it! Gads my life if I
thought it were so, I would this moment renounce all
communication with you. Ungrateful monster! He? Is it so?   35
Ay, I see it, a plot upon my honour; your guilty cheeks
confess it; oh where shall wronged virtue fly for reparation?
I'll be divorced this instant.

SIR PAUL
Gadsbud, what shall I say? This is the strangest surprise!
Why I don't know anything at all, nor I don't know whether   40
there be anything at all in the world, or no.

LADY PLYANT
I thought I should try you, false man. I that never
dissembled in my life: yet to make trial of you, pretended to
like that monster of iniquity, Careless, and found out that
contrivance to let you see this letter; which now I find was   45
of your own inditing—I do, heathen, I do; see my face no

19 *have been* Q2 (even been Q1)
19-20 *and rendered...nature* Q1 (*om.* W1)
32-3 S.D. so, Ed. (*indented* Q1; *follows* here? W1)

---

19 *been even.* Q2's word-order achieves a more satisfactory placing of emphasis.
24-5 *you were...water.* Cf. 'The very ice of chastity is in them' (*As You Like It*,
    III,iv. 18); and 'She was false as water' (*Othello*, V,ii. 135)

more; there has hardly been consummation between us, and
I'll be divorced presently.

SIR PAUL
Oh strange, what will become of me?—I'm so amazed, and
so overjoyed, so afraid, and so sorry.—But did you give me 50
this letter on purpose, he? Did you?

LADY PLYANT
Did I? Do you doubt me, Turk, Saracen? I have a cousin
that's a proctor in the Commons, I'll go to him instantly.—

SIR PAUL
Hold, stay, I beseech your ladyship—I'm so overjoyed, stay,
I'll confess all. 55

LADY PLYANT
What will you confess, Jew?

SIR PAUL
Why now as I hope to be saved, I had no hand in this
letter—nay hear me, I beseech your ladyship: the devil take
me now if he did not go beyond my commission—if I
desired him to do any more than speak a good word only 60
just for me, gadsbud only for poor Sir Paul, I'm an
Anabaptist, or a Jew, or what you please to call me.

LADY PLYANT
Why, is not here matter of fact?

SIR PAUL
Ay, but by your own virtue and continency that matter of
fact is all his own doing.—I confess I had a great desire to 65
have some honours conferred upon me, which lie all in your
ladyship's breast, and he being a well-spoken man, I desired
him to intercede for me.—

LADY PLYANT
Did you so, Presumption! Well, remember, for this, your
right hand shall be swathed down again tonight—and I 70
thought to have always allowed you that liberty—

SIR PAUL
Nay but madam, I shall offend again if you don't allow me
that to reach—

47 *there...and* Q1 (*om.* W1)
53 *proctor in the Commons* officer who managed causes in court involving
  dissolution of marriage, probate, etc., in the Doctors' Commons buildings in
  London
57 *hope* Q1 (hoped W2)
69-74 *Well. . .bed.* Q1 (Oh! He comes, the Tarquin comes; I cannot bear his sight.
  W1)

LADY PLYANT

Drink the less you sot, and do't before you come to bed.

Exit

Enter CARELESS

CARELESS

Sir Paul, I'm glad I've met with you; 'gad I have said all I   75
could, but can't prevail—then my friendship to you has
carried me a little farther in this matter—

SIR PAUL

Indeed—well, sir?—(*Aside*) I'll dissemble with him a little.

CARELESS

Why faith I have in my time known honest gentlemen
abused by a pretended coyness in their wives, and I had a   80
mind to try my lady's virtue—and when I could not prevail
for you, 'gad I pretended to be in love myself—but all in
vain, she would not hear a word upon that subject: then I
writ a letter to her; I don't know what effects that will have,
but I'll be sure to tell you when I do, though by this light I   85
believe her virtue is impregnable.

SIR PAUL

Oh Providence! Providence! What discoveries are here
made! Why, this is better and more miraculous than the
rest.

CARELESS

What do you mean?   90

SIR PAUL

I can't tell you, I'm so overjoyed; come along with me to my
lady, I can't contain myself; come my dear friend.

CARELESS (*Aside*)

So, so, so, this difficulty's over.   *Exeunt*

[Act IV, Scene v]

Enter MELLEFONT *and* MASKWELL *severally*

MELLEFONT

Maskwell! I have been looking for you—'tis within a
quarter of eight.

MASKWELL

My lady is just gone down from my lord's closet; you had

3 *down from* Q1 (into Q2)

---

3 *down from.* Q2's 'into' is presumably a mistake. Lady Touchwood has been in
her husband's closet since midway through Act III, and is now going downstairs
to meet 'the company'.

best steal into her chamber before she comes, and lie
concealed there, otherwise she may lock the door when we   5
are together, and you not easily get in to surprise us.

MELLEFONT

He? You say true.

MASKWELL

You had best make haste, for after she has made some
apology to the company for her own, and my lord's absence
all this while, she'll retire to her chamber instantly.   10

MELLEFONT

I go this moment: now Fortune I defy thee.   *Exit*

MASKWELL

I confess you may be allowed to be secure in your own
opinion; the appearance is very fair, but I have an after-
game to play that shall turn the tables, and here comes the
man that I must manage.   15

Enter LORD TOUCHWOOD

LORD TOUCHWOOD

Maskwell, you are the man I wished to meet.

MASKWELL

I am happy to be in the way of your lordship's commands.

LORD TOUCHWOOD

I have always found you prudent and careful in anything
that has concerned me or my family.

MASKWELL

I were a villain else—I am bound by duty and gratitude, and   20
my own inclination, to be ever your lordship's servant.

LORD TOUCHWOOD

Enough—you are my friend; I know it: yet there has been a
thing in your knowledge, which has concerned me nearly,
that you have concealed from me.

MASKWELL

My lord!   25

LORD TOUCHWOOD

Nay, I excuse your friendship to my unnatural nephew thus
far—but I know you have been privy to his impious designs
upon my wife. This evening she has told me all: her good
nature concealed it as long as was possible; but he
preserves so in villainy, that she has told me even you were   30
weary of dissuading him, though you have once actually
hindered him from forcing her.

8 *after she has made* W1 (she's but gone to make Q1; she's gone to make Q2)
10 *she'll retire* W1 (and will Q1)

MASKWELL

>I am sorry, my lord, I can make you no answer; this is an
>occasion in which I would not willingly be so silent.

LORD TOUCHWOOD

>I know you would excuse him—and I know as well that you   35
>can't.

MASKWELL

>Indeed I was in hopes 't had been a youthful heat that might
>have soon boiled over; but—

LORD TOUCHWOOD

>Say on.

MASKWELL

>I have nothing more to say, my lord—but to express my   40
>concern; for I think his frenzy increases daily.

LORD TOUCHWOOD

>How! Give me but proof of it, ocular proof, that I may
>justify my dealing with him to the world, and share my
>fortunes.

MASKWELL

>Oh my lord! Consider that is hard: besides, time may work   45
>upon him: then, for me to do it! I have professed an
>everlasting friendship to him.

LORD TOUCHWOOD

>He is your friend, and what am I?

MASKWELL

>I am answered.

LORD TOUCHWOOD

>Fear not his displeasure; I will put you out of his, and   50
>Fortune's power, and for that thou art scrupulously honest,
>I will secure thy fidelity to him, and give my honour never
>to own any discovery that you shall make me. Can you give
>me a demonstrative proof? Speak.

MASKWELL

>I wish I could not—to be plain, my lord, I intended this   55
>evening to have tried all arguments to dissuade him from a
>design, which I suspect; and if I had not succeeded, to have
>informed your lordship of what I knew.

---

34 *so* Q1 (*om.* W1)
31 *can...no* Q1 (can't make you an Q2)

8-10 *after. . .retire.* W1's changes shift the sentence to a syntactic structure.
42 *Give. . .proof.* He echoes Othello's demand to Iago, 'give me the ocular proof'
(III,iii. 366).

LORD TOUCHWOOD

I thank you. What is the villain's purpose?

MASKWELL

He has owned nothing to me of late, and what I mean now,   60
is only a bare suspicion of my own. If your lordship will
meet me a quarter of an hour hence there, in that lobby by
my lady's bedchamber, I shall be able to tell you more.

LORD TOUCHWOOD

I will.

MASKWELL

My duty to your lordship makes me do a severe piece of   65
justice.—

LORD TOUCHWOOD

I will be secret, and reward your honesty beyond your
hopes.   *Exeunt severally*

[Act IV, Scene vi]

SCENE opening shows LADY TOUCHWOOD's *Chamber*
MELLEFONT, *solus*

MELLEFONT

Pray Heaven my aunt keep touch with her assignation.—Oh
that her lord were but sweating behind this hanging, with
the expectation of what I shall see—hist, she comes—little
does she think what a mine is just ready to spring under her
feet. But to my post.   *Goes behind the hangings*   5

Enter LADY TOUCHWOOD

LADY TOUCHWOOD

'Tis eight o'clock: methinks I should have found him here.
Who does not prevent the hour of love, outstays the time;
for to be dully punctual is too slow.—

Enter MASKWELL

I was accusing you of neglect.

MASKWELL

I confess you do reproach me when I see you here before   10

5 *hangings* Q2, W1 (hanging Q1, W2)
7 *prevent* anticipate

0.02 *SCENE opening.* In the Restoration theatre, the back-scene for the gallery
would have been painted on two shutters, which are here drawn apart to expose
the bed-chamber set.

me; but 'tis fit I should be still behindhand, still to be more
and more indebted to your goodness.

LADY TOUCHWOOD

You can excuse a fault too well, not to have been to
blame—a ready answer shows you were prepared.

MASKWELL

Guilt is ever at a loss and confusion waits upon it, when   15
innocence and bold truth are always ready for expression—

LADY TOUCHWOOD

Not in love; words are the weak support of cold
indifference; love has no language to be heard.

MASKWELL

Excess of joy had made me stupid! Thus may my lips be
ever closed. (*Kisses her*) And thus—oh who would not lose   20
his speech, upon condition to have joys above it?

LADY TOUCHWOOD

Hold, let me lock the door first.   *Goes to the door*

MASKWELL (*Aside*)

That I believed; 'twas well I left the private passage open.

LADY TOUCHWOOD

So, that's safe.

MASKWELL

And so may all your pleasures be, and secret as this kiss—   25

MELLEFONT (*Leaps out*)

And may all treachery be thus discovered.

LADY TOUCHWOOD (*Shrieks*)

Ah!

MELLEFONT (*Offers to draw*)

Villain!

MASKWELL

Nay then, there's but one way.   *Runs out*

MELLEFONT

Say you so, were you provided for an escape? Hold, madam,   30
you have no more holes to your burrow, I'll stand between
you and this sally-port.

LADY TOUCHWOOD

Thunder strike thee dead for this deceit, immediate
lightning blast thee, me and the whole world—oh! I could
rack myself, play the vulture to my own heart, and gnaw it   35
piecemeal, for not boding to me this misfortune.

19 *had* Q1 (has Q2)

34-6 I. . .piecemeal. She echoes Roxana in *The Rival Queens:* 'O I cou'd tear my
flesh, Or him, or you, nay all the world to pieces' (IV,i. 117-8); and Statira to
Roxana: 'Feed like a Vulture, tear my bleeding heart' (V,i.104).

MELLEFONT
> Be patient.—

LADY TOUCHWOOD
> Be damned.

MELLEFONT
> Consider I have you on the hook; you will but flounder
> yourself a-weary, and be nevertheless my prisoner.　　　40

LADY TOUCHWOOD
> I'll hold my breath and die, but I'll be free.

MELLEFONT
> Oh madam, have a care of dying unprepared, I doubt you
> have some unrepented sins that may hang heavy, and retard
> your flight.

LADY TOUCHWOOD
> Oh! What shall I do? Say? Whither shall I turn? Has hell no　　45
> remedy?

MELLEFONT
> None, hell has served you even as heaven has done, left you
> to yourself.—You're in a kind of Erasmus' paradise; yet if
> you please you may make it a purgatory; and with a little
> penance and my absolution all this may turn to good　　50
> account.

LADY TOUCHWOOD (*Aside*)
> Hold in my passion, and fall, fall a little thou swelling
> heart; let me have some intermission of this rage, and one
> minute's coolness to dissemble.　　　　　　　*She weeps*

MELLEFONT
> You have been to blame.—I like those tears, and hope they　　55
> are of the purest kind—penitential tears.

LADY TOUCHWOOD
> Oh the scene was shifted quick before me—I had not time to
> think—I was surprised to see a monster in the glass, and
> now I find 'tis myself; can you have mercy to forgive the
> faults I have imagined, but never put into practice?—Oh　　60

---

59 *'tis* W1 (it is Q1)

47-8 *hell. . .paradise.* See Longer Notes, No. 4.

57 *the scene. . .me.* The idea is, doubtless, that as in the scene-change just
witnessed, the previous scene (worldly appearance, or immoral obsession)
'opens' to reveal the new scene (moral reality) behind it.

58-9 *a monster. . .myself.* (a) The new scene is a morally revealing mirror, in which
she (ostensibly) sees a 'monster'; cf. the proverb, 'He that beholds himself in a
glass, may see himself well,' Tilley G133; *Hamlet,* III,iv.19-20; (b) the 'monster'
may be a demon; see II.29-31n.

59 *'tis.* W1 here tightens the rhythm, and focusses the emphasis.

consider, consider how fatal you have been to me, you have
already killed the quiet of this life. The love of you was the
first wandering fire that e'er misled my steps, and while I
had only that in view, I was betrayed into unthought-of
ways of ruin.   65

MELLEFONT

May I believe this true?

LADY TOUCHWOOD

Oh be not cruelly incredulous—how can you doubt these
streaming eyes? Keep the severest eye o'er all my future
conduct; and if I once relapse, let me not hope forgiveness;
'twill ever be in your power to ruin me—my lord shall sign   70
to your desires; I will myself create your happiness, and
Cynthia shall be this night your bride—do but conceal my
failings, and forgive.

MELLEFONT

Upon such terms I will be ever yours in every honest way.

Enter LORD TOUCHWOOD, MASKWELL *softly behind him*

MASKWELL

I have kept my word, he's here, but I must not be seen. *Exit*   75

LORD TOUCHWOOD

Hell and amazement, she's in tears.

LADY TOUCHWOOD (*Kneeling*)

Eternal blessings thank you—(*Aside*) Ha! My lord listening!
Oh Fortune has o'erpaid me all! All, all's my own!

MELLEFONT

Nay, I beseech you rise.

LADY TOUCHWOOD (*Aloud*)

Never, never! I'll grow to the ground, be buried quick   80
beneath it, ere I'll be consenting to so damned a sin as
incest! Unnatural incest!

MELLEFONT

Ha!

LADY TOUCHWOOD

Oh cruel man, will you not let me go?—I'll forgive all that's
past—oh heaven, you will not ravish me?   85

MELLEFONT

Damnation!

74.1 *Enter...him* Q1 (MASKWELL *softly introduces* LORD TOUCHWOOD, *and retires*
W1)
81 *I'll* Q2 (I Q1)

81 *I'll.* Q1's 'I' is possible, but incorrect and awkward.

LORD TOUCHWOOD

Monster, dog! Your life shall answer this—

Draws, and runs at MELLEFONT, *is held by* LADY TOUCHWOOD

LADY TOUCHWOOD

Oh heavens, my lord! Hold, hold, for heaven's sake.

MELLEFONT

Confusion, my uncle! Oh the damned sorceress!

LADY TOUCHWOOD

Moderate your rage, good my lord! He's mad, alas he's   90
mad—indeed he is, my lord, and knows not what he
does—see how wild he looks.

MELLEFONT

By heaven 'twere senseless not to be mad, and see such
witchcraft.

LADY TOUCHWOOD

My lord, you hear him, he talks idly.   95

LORD TOUCHWOOD

Hence from my sight, thou living infamy to my name;
when next I see that face, I'll write villain in't with my
sword's point.

MELLEFONT

Now, by my soul, I will not go till I have made known my
wrongs—nay, till I have made known yours, which (if   100
possible) are greater—though she has all the host of hell her
servants; though she can wear more shapes in shining day,
than fear shows cowards in the dark—

LADY TOUCHWOOD

Alas he raves! Talks very poetry! For heaven's sake away,
my lord, he'll either tempt you to extravagance, or commit 105
some himself.

MELLEFONT

Death and furies, will you not hear me?—Why by heaven
she laughs, grins, points to your back; she forks out
cuckoldom with her fingers, and you're running horn-mad
after your fortune.   110

          As she is going she turns back and smiles at him

LORD TOUCHWOOD

I fear he's mad indeed—let's send Maskwell to him.

MELLEFONT

Send him to her.

91 *he is* Q2 (he's Q1)
95 *idly* deliriously
101-3 *though. . .dark* Q1 (*om.* W1)

91 *he is.* Q2's expansion is clearly needed to convey the intended sense.

LADY TOUCHWOOD
  Come, come, good my lord, my heart aches so, I shall faint
  if I stay.   *Exeunt* LORD *and* LADY TOUCHWOOD
MELLEFONT
  Oh I could curse my stars, fate, and chance; all causes and   115
  accidents of fortune in this life! But to what purpose? Yet,
  'sdeath, for a man to have the fruit of all his industry grow
  full and ripe, ready to drop into his mouth, and just when
  he holds out his hand to gather it, to have a sudden
  whirlwind come, tear up tree and all, and bear away the   120
  very root and foundation of his hopes; what temper can
  contain? They talk of sending Maskwell to me; I never had
  more need of him—but what can he do? Imagination cannot
  form a fairer and more plausible design than this of his
  which has miscarried.—Oh my precious aunt, I shall never   125
  thrive without I deal with the devil, or another woman.
          Women like flames have a destroying power,
          Ne'er to be quenched, till they themselves devour.
                                                      Exit

                    SCENE shuts

                    Act V, Scene i

                    [*The Gallery*]
            Enter LADY TOUCHWOOD *and* MASKWELL

LADY TOUCHWOOD
  Was't not lucky?
MASKWELL
  Lucky! Fortune is your own, and 'tis her interest so to be;
  by heaven I believe you can control her power, and she
  fears it; though chance brought my lord, 'twas your own art
  that turned it to advantage.   5
LADY TOUCHWOOD
  'Tis true it might have been my ruin—but yonder's my
  lord, I believe he's coming to find you, I'll not be seen. *Exit*
MASKWELL
  So; I durst not own my introducing my lord, though it
  succeeded well for her, for she would have suspected a
  design which I should have been puzzled to excuse. My   10

117 *grow* Q2 (grown Q1)
_____

117 *grow.* This has the advantage, over Q1's 'grown', of continuing activity.

lord is thoughtful—I'll be so too; yet he shall know my thoughts; or think he does—

Enter LORD TOUCHWOOD

MASKWELL
What have I done?

LORD TOUCHWOOD [*Aside*]
Talking to himself!

MASKWELL
'Twas honest—and shall I be rewarded for it? No, 'twas honest, therefore I shan't;—nay, rather therefore I ought not; for it rewards itself.   15

LORD TOUCHWOOD (*Aside*)
Unequalled virtue!

MASKWELL
But should it be known? Then I have lost a friend! He was an ill man, and I have gained; for half myself I lent him, and that I have recalled; so I have served myself, and what is yet better I have served a worthy lord to whom I owe myself.   20

LORD TOUCHWOOD (*Aside*)
Excellent man!

MASKWELL
Yet I am wretched—oh there is a secret burns within this breast, which should it once blaze forth, would ruin all, consume my honest character, and brand me with the name of villain.   25

LORD TOUCHWOOD [*Aside*]
Ha!

MASKWELL
Why do I love? Yet heaven and my waking conscience are my witnesses, I never gave one working thought a vent, which might discover that I loved, nor ever must; no, let it prey upon my heart; for I would rather die, than seem once, barely seem, dishonest:—oh, should it once be known I love fair Cynthia, all this that I have done would look like rival's malice, false friendship to my lord, and base self-interest. Let me perish first, and from this hour avoid all sight and speech, and, if I can, all thought of that pernicious beauty. Ha! But what is my distraction doing? I am wildly talking to   30

                               35

15-17 *'Twas honest...itself.* Proverbial, 'Virtue is its own reward,' Tilley V81; possibly recalling Seneca: 'Do you ask what I seek in virtue? Only herself. For she offers nothing better—she herself is her own reward, *De Vita Beata*, IX, 4.

myself, and some ill chance might have directed malicious
ears this way.   *Seems to start, seeing my lord*   40

LORD TOUCHWOOD

Start not—let guilty and dishonest souls start at the
revelation of their thoughts, but be thou fixed, as is thy
virtue.

MASKWELL

I am confounded, and beg your lordship's pardon for those
free discourses which I have had with myself.   45

LORD TOUCHWOOD

Come, I beg your pardon that I overheard you, and yet it
shall not need.—Honest Maskwell! Thy and my good genius
led me hither—mine, in that I have discovered so much
manly virtue; thine, in that thou shalt have due reward of
all thy worth. Give me thy hand—my nephew is the alone   50
remaining branch of all our ancient family; him I thus blow
away, and constitute thee in his room to be my heir—

MASKWELL

Now heaven forbid—

LORD TOUCHWOOD

No more—I have resolved—the writings are ready drawn,
and wanted nothing but to be signed, and have his name   55
inserted—yours will fill the blank as well—I will have no
reply—let me command this time; for 'tis the last, in which
I will assume authority—hereafter, you shall rule where I
have power.

MASKWELL

I humbly would petition—   60

LORD TOUCHWOOD

Is't for yourself?—(MASKWELL *pauses*) I'll hear of nought
for anybody else.

MASKWELL

Then witness heaven for me, this wealth and honour was
not of my seeking, nor would I build my fortune on
another's ruin: I had but one desire—   65

LORD TOUCHWOOD

Thou shalt enjoy it—if all I'm worth in wealth or interest
can purchase Cynthia, she is thine.—I'm sure Sir Paul's
consent will follow fortune; I'll quickly show him which
way that is going.

MASKWELL

You oppress me with bounty; my gratitude is weak, and   70

51-2 *him I thus blow away.* Echoing Othello's 'All my fond love thus do I blow to
heaven' (*Othello*; III,iii. 452).

shrinks beneath the weight, and cannot rise to thank
you—what, enjoy my love! Forgive the transports of a
blessing so unexpected, so unhoped for, so unthought of!

LORD TOUCHWOOD

I will confirm it, and rejoice with thee.   *Exit*

MASKWELL

This is prosperous indeed—why, let him find me out a   75
villain, settled in possession of a fair estate, and full fruition
of my love, I'll bear the railings of a losing gamester—but
should he find me out before? 'Tis dangerous to delay—let
me think—should my lord proceed to treat openly of my
marriage with Cynthia, all must be discovered, and   80
Mellefont can be no longer blinded.—It must not be; nay,
should my lady know it—ay, then were fine work indeed!
Her fury would spare nothing, though she involved herself
in ruin. No, it must be by stratagem—I must deceive
Mellefont once more, and get my lord to consent to my   85
private management. He comes opportunely—now will I, in
my old way, discover the whole and real truth of the matter
to him, that he may not suspect one word on't.

> No mask like open truth to cover lies,
> As to go naked is the best disguise.   90

Enter MELLEFONT

MELLEFONT

Oh Maskwell, what hopes? I am confounded in a maze of
thoughts, each leading into one another, and all ending in
perplexity. My uncle will not see, nor hear me.

MASKWELL

No matter, sir, don't trouble your head, all's in my power.

MELLEFONT

How, for heaven's sake?   95

MASKWELL

Little do you think that your aunt has kept her word,—how
the devil she wrought my lord into this dotage, I know not;
but he's gone to Sir Paul about my marriage with Cynthia,
and has appointed me his heir.

MELLEFONT

The devil he has! What's to be done?   100

MASKWELL

I have it, it must be by stratagem; for it's in vain to make
application to him. I think I have that in my head that
cannot fail: where's Cynthia?

MELLEFONT

In the garden.

MASKWELL

    Let us go and consult her; my life for yours, I cheat my   105
lord.   *Exeunt*

[Act V, Scene ii]

Enter LORD TOUCHWOOD, LADY TOUCHWOOD

LADY TOUCHWOOD

    Maskwell your heir, and marry Cynthia!

LORD TOUCHWOOD

    I cannot do too much for so much merit.

LADY TOUCHWOOD

    But this is a thing of too great moment to be so suddenly
resolved. Why Cynthia? Why must he be married? Is there
not reward enough in raising his low fortune, but he must   5
mix his blood with mine, and wed my niece? How know
you that my brother will consent, or she? Nay, he himself
perhaps may have affections otherwhere.

LORD TOUCHWOOD

    No, I am convinced he loves her.

LADY TOUCHWOOD

    Maskwell love Cynthia, impossible!   10

LORD TOUCHWOOD

    I told you, he confessed it to me.

LADY TOUCHWOOD (*Aside*)

    Confusion! How's this?

LORD TOUCHWOOD

    His humility long stifled his passion: and his love of
Mellefont would have made him still conceal it.—But by
encouragement, I wrung the secret from him; and know   15
he's no way to be rewarded but in her. I'll defer my farther
proceedings in it, till you have considered it; but remember
how we are both indebted to him.   *Exit*

LADY TOUCHWOOD

    Both indebted to him! Yes, we are both indebted to him, if
you knew all, damned villain! Oh, I am wild with this   20
surprise of treachery: hell and fire, it is impossible, it
cannot be!—He love Cynthia! What, have I been bawd to
his designs, his property only, a baiting place to stay his

11 *told* Q1 (tell W1)
20 *damned* Q1 (*om.* W1)
23 *property* tool

stomach in the road to her? Now I see what made him false
to Mellefont.—Shame and distraction! I cannot bear it. Oh!   25
What woman can bear to be a property? To be kindled to a
flame, only to light him to another's arms? Oh! That I were
fire indeed, that I might burn the vile traitor to a hell of
torments,—but he's damnation proof, a devil already, and
fire is his element. What shall I do? How shall I think? I   30
cannot think,—all my designs are lost, my love unsated, my
revenge unfinished, and fresh cause of fury from
unthought-of plagues.

Enter SIR PAUL

SIR PAUL
Madam, sister, my lady sister, did you see my lady my wife?
LADY TOUCHWOOD
Oh! Torture!   35
SIR PAUL
Gadsbud, I can't find her high nor low; where can she be,
think you?
LADY TOUCHWOOD
Where she's serving you, as all your sex ought to be served:
making you a beast. Don't you know that you're a fool,
brother?   40
SIR PAUL
A fool; he, he, he, you're merry—no, no, not I, I know no
such matter.
LADY TOUCHWOOD
Why then you don't know half your happiness.
SIR PAUL
That's a jest with all my heart, faith and troth,—but
hark'ee, my lord told me something of a revolution of   45
things; I don't know what to make on't,—gadsbud I must
consult my wife,—he talks of disinheriting his nephew; and
I don't know what,—look you, sister, I must know what my
girl has to trust to; or not a syllable of a wedding,
gadsbud—to show you that I am not a fool.   50
LADY TOUCHWOOD
Hear me; consent to the breaking off this marriage, and the

23-4 *to stay. . .her* Q1 (*om.* W1)
25 *distraction* W1 (destruction Q1)
28-30 *to. . .element* Q1 (*om.* W1)
38 *all* Q1, W1 (*om.* Q2)

25 *distraction.* 'Insanity' fits and reinforces the context.

promoting any other, without consulting me, and I'll
renounce all blood, all relation and concern with you for
ever,—nay, I'll be your enemy, and pursue you to
destruction, I'll tear your eyes out, and tread you under my   55
feet.—

SIR PAUL

Why, what's the matter now? Good Lord, what's all this
for? Pooh, here's a joke indeed—why, where's my wife?

LADY TOUCHWOOD

With Careless, in the close arbour; he may want you by this
time, as much as you want her.   60

SIR PAUL

Oh, if she be with Mr. Careless, 'tis well enough.

LADY TOUCHWOOD

Fool, sot, insensible ox! But remember what I said to you,
or you had better eat your own horns, and pimp for your
living; by this light you had.   *Exit*

SIR PAUL

She's a passionate woman, gadsbud,—but to say truth, all   65
our family are choleric; I am the only peaceable person
amongst 'em.   *Exit*

[Act V, Scene iii]

Enter MELLEFONT, MASKWELL, *and* CYNTHIA

MELLEFONT

I know no other way but this he has proposed; if you have
love enough to run the venture.

CYNTHIA

I don't know whether I have love enough,—but I find I have
obstinacy enough to pursue whatever I have once resolved;
and a true female courage to oppose anything that resists   5
my will, though 'twere reason itself.

MASKWELL

That's right,—well, I'll secure the writings, and run the
hazard along with you.

CYNTHIA

But how can the coach and six horses be got ready without
suspicion?   10

59 *close* enclosed, secluded
63 *own* Q1, W1 (*om.* Q2)
63-4 *and. . .living* Q1 (*om.* W1)
65 *She's* Q1 (You're W1)

MASKWELL

Leave it to my care; that shall be so far from being
suspected, that it shall be got ready by my lord's own order.

MELLEFONT

How?

MASKWELL

Why, I intend to tell my lord the whole matter of our
contrivance, that's my way.   15

MELLEFONT

I don't understand you.

MASKWELL

Why, I'll tell my lord, I laid this plot with you, on purpose
to betray you; and that which put me upon it, was, the
finding it impossible to gain the lady any other way, but in
the hopes of her marrying you.   20

MELLEFONT

So?—

MASKWELL

So, why so, while you're busied in making yourself ready,
I'll wheedle her into the coach; and instead of you, borrow
my lord's chaplain, and so run away with her myself.

MELLEFONT

Oh I conceive you, you'll tell him so?   25

MASKWELL

Tell him so! Ay; why you don't think I mean to do so?

MELLEFONT

No, no; ha, ha, I dare swear thou wilt not.

MASKWELL

(Aside) You may be deceived.—[To them] Therefore for our
farther security, I would have you disguised like a parson,
that if my lord should have curiosity to peep, he may not   30
discover you in the coach, but think the cheat is carried on
as he would have it.

MELLEFONT

Excellent Maskwell! Thou wert certainly meant for a
statesman or a Jesuit, but that thou'rt too honest for one,
and too pious for the other.   35

MASKWELL

Well, get yourselves ready, and meet me in half an hour,

---

22 *you're* W1 (you are Q1)
28 *(Aside) You may be deceived.*—Q1 (*om.* W1)
34 *that thou'rt* Q1 (thou art W1)

---

22 *you're.* W1 here tightens the rhythm.

yonder in my lady's dressing-room; go by the back stairs,
and so we may slip down without being observed.—I'll send
the chaplain to you with his robes; I have made him my
own,—and ordered him to meet us tomorrow morning at St.　40
Albans; there we will sum up this account, to all our
satisfactions.

MELLEFONT

Should I begin to thank or praise thee, I should waste the
little time we have.　　　　　　　　　　　　　　　　　*Exit*

MASKWELL

Madam, you will be ready?　　　　　　　　　　　　　　　45

CYNTHIA

I will be punctual to the minute.　　　　　　　　　*Going*

MASKWELL

Stay, I have a doubt—upon second thoughts, we had better
meet in the chaplain's chamber here, the corner chamber at
this end of the gallery, there is a back way into it, so that
you need not come through this door—and a pair of private　50
stairs leading down to the stables—it will be more
convenient.

CYNTHIA

I am guided by you—but Mellefont will mistake.

MASKWELL

No, no, I'll after him immediately, and tell him.

CYNTHIA

I will not fail.　　　　　　　　　　　　　　　　　*Exit*　55

MASKWELL

Why, *qui vult decipi decipiatur.*—'Tis no fault of mine, I
have told 'em in plain terms, how easy 'tis for me to cheat
'em; and if they will not hear the serpent's hiss, they must
be stung into experience, and future caution.—Now to
prepare my lord to consent to this.—But first I must　60
instruct my little Levite; there is no plot, public or private,
that can expect to prosper without one of them has a finger
in't. He promised me to be within at this hour,—Mr.
Saygrace, Mr. Saygrace. *Goes to the chamber door, and knocks*

---

51 *leading* W1 (leads Q1)
61 *Levite* domestic chaplain (somewhat contemptuous)
62 *them has* W1 ('em have Q1; 'em has Q2)

---

51 *leading.* W1's participle better coordinates the sentence.
56 *qui vult decipi, decipiatur.* 'Who wish to be deceived, let them be deceived' (ex.
　　Cardinal Carlo Garaffa: *'Populus vult,'* etc.).
58-9 *and if...caution.* Cf. II. 394-5n. and note.
62 *them has.* The construction needs the strength of W1's 'them.'

SAYGRACE (*Looking out*)

Sweet sir, I will but pen the last line of an acrostic, and be   65
with you in the twinkling of an ejaculation, in the
pronouncing of an Amen, or before you can—

MASKWELL

Nay, good Mr. Saygrace do not prolong the time, by
describing to me the shortness of your stay; rather if you
please, defer the finishing of your wit, and let us talk about   70
our business, it shall be tithes in your way.

SAYGRACE (*Enters*)

You shall prevail, I would break off in the middle of a
sermon to do you a pleasure.

MASKWELL

You could not do me a greater,—except—the business in   75
hand—have you provided a habit for Mellefont?

SAYGRACE

I have, they are ready in my chamber, together with a clean
starched band and cuffs.

MASKWELL

Good, let them be carried to him,—have you stitched the
gown sleeve, that he may be puzzled, and waste time in   80
putting it on?

SAYGRACE

I have; the gown will not be endued without perplexity.

MASKWELL

Meet me in half an hour, here in your own chamber. When
Cynthia comes, let there be no light, and do not speak, that
she may not distinguish you from Mellefont. I'll urge haste,   85
to excuse your silence.

SAYGRACE

You have no more commands.

MASKWELL

None, your text is short.

SAYGRACE

But pithy, and I will handle it with discretion.   *Exit*

MASKWELL

It will be the first you have so served.

Enter LORD TOUCHWOOD

---

66 *ejaculation* short prayer
73 *a pleasure* W1 (pleasure Q1)

---

73 *a pleasure.* The following speech requires that the reference be to some specific
favour.

LORD TOUCHWOOD

Sure I was born to be controlled by those I should   90
command: my very slaves will shortly give me rules how I
shall govern them.

MASKWELL

I am concerned to see your lordship discomposed—

LORD TOUCHWOOD

Have you seen my wife lately, or disobliged her?

MASKWELL

No, my lord. (*Aside*) What can this mean?   95

LORD TOUCHWOOD

Then Mellefont has urged somebody to incense her
—something she has heard of you which carries her beyond
the bounds of patience.

MASKWELL

(*Aside*) This I feared. [*To him*] Did not your lordship tell
her of the honours you designed me?   100

LORD TOUCHWOOD

Yes.

MASKWELL

'Tis that; you know my lady has a high spirit; she thinks I
am unworthy.

LORD TOUCHWOOD

Unworthy! 'Tis an ignorant pride in her to think so
—honesty to me is true nobility. However, 'tis my will it   105
shall be so, and that should be convincing to her as much as
reason—by heaven, I'll not be wife-ridden; were it possible,
it should be done this night.

MASKWELL

(*Aside*) By heaven he meets my wishes. [*To him*] Few things
are impossible to willing minds.   110

LORD TOUCHWOOD

Instruct me how this may be done, you shall see I want no
inclination.

MASKWELL

I had laid a small design for tomorrow (as love will be
inventing) which I thought to communicate to your
lordship—but it may be as well done tonight.   115

LORD TOUCHWOOD

Here's company—come this way, and tell me.   *Exeunt*

---

105 *honesty. . .nobility* proverbial, Tilley V85, 'Virtue is the true nobility'
106 *shall* W1 (should Q1)

---

106 *shall.* This is more positive than 'should' and avoids repetition.

[Act V, Scene iv]

Enter CARELESS *and* CYNTHIA

CARELESS

Is not that he, now gone out with my lord?

CYNTHIA

Yes.

CARELESS

By heaven there's treachery—the confusion that I saw your
father in, my Lady Touchwood's passion, with what
imperfectly I overheard between my lord and her, confirm   5
me in my fears. Where's Mellefont?

CYNTHIA

Here he comes.

Enter MELLEFONT

Did Maskwell tell you anything of the chaplain's chamber?

MELLEFONT

No; my dear, will you get ready?—The things are all in my
chamber; I want nothing but the habit.   10

CARELESS

You are betrayed, and Maskwell is the villain I always
thought him.

CYNTHIA

When you were gone, he said his mind was changed, and
bid me meet him in the chaplain's room, pretending
immediately to follow you, and give you notice.   15

MELLEFONT

How?

CARELESS

There's Saygrace tripping by with a bundle under his
arm—he cannot be ignorant that Maskwell means to use his
chamber; let's follow and examine him.

MELLEFONT

'Tis loss of time—I cannot think him false.   20

Exeunt MELLEFONT *and* CARELESS

CYNTHIA

My lord musing!

---

11 *I* Q2 (that I Q1)

11 *I.* The deletion of Q1's 'that' sharpens the speech-rhythm.
17 *There's Saygrace.* He probably passes across the stage at this point, taking the
habit from his chamber to Mellefont's; alternatively, he might be offstage but
visible to Careless.

Enter LORD TOUCHWOOD

LORD TOUCHWOOD [*Not seeing her*]
He has a quick invention, if this were suddenly
designed—yet he says he had prepared my chaplain already.

CYNTHIA
How's this? Now I fear indeed.

LORD TOUCHWOOD
Cynthia here; alone, fair cousin, and melancholy? 25

CYNTHIA
Your lordship was thoughtful.

LORD TOUCHWOOD
My thoughts were on serious business, not worth your
hearing.

CYNTHIA
Mine were on treachery concerning you, and may be worth
your hearing. 30

LORD TOUCHWOOD
Treachery concerning me! Pray be plain—hark! What
noise?

MASKWELL (*Within*)
Will you not hear me?

LADY TOUCHWOOD (*Within*)
No, monster! Hellish traitor! No!

CYNTHIA
My lady and Maskwell! This may be lucky—my lord, let 35
me entreat you to stand behind this screen, and listen;
perhaps this chance may give you proof of what you ne'er
could have believed from my suspicions.

CYNTHIA *and* LORD TOUCHWOOD *abscond, listening*

Enter LADY TOUCHWOOD *with a dagger,* MASKWELL

LADY TOUCHWOOD
You want but leisure to invent fresh falsehood, and soothe
me to a fond belief of all your fictions; but I will stab the lie 40

34 *Hellish* Q1 (*om.* W1)
38.1 CYNTHIA. . .*listening* W1 (*They abscond* Q1)

---

36 *behind this screen.* A frontispiece illustration first observed in the 1733 edition of
the play shows the following sequence, with Maskwell and Lady Touchwood
on the forestage, Cynthia and Lord Touchwood listening, not from behind a
screen but from behind the edge of the drawn stage-curtain, at stage-left.
Avoiding the use of a screen has clear advantages in relation to the Act IV scene
vi scene change.

that's forming in your heart, and save a sin, in pity to your
soul.

MASKWELL

Strike then—since you will have it so.

LADY TOUCHWOOD

Ha! A steady villain to the last!

MASKWELL

Come, why do you dally with me thus?   45

LADY TOUCHWOOD

Thy stubborn temper shocks me, and you knew it
would—by heaven, this is cunning all, and not courage; no,
I know thee well: but thou shalt miss thy aim.

MASKWELL

Ha, ha, ha.

LADY TOUCHWOOD

Ha! Do you mock my rage? Then this shall punish your   50
fond, rash contempt! Again smile!   *Goes to strike*
And such a smile as speaks in ambiguity!
Tenthousandmeaningslurkineachcornerofthatvariousface,
Oh! That they were written in thy heart,
That I, with this, might lay thee open to my sight!   55
But then 'twill be too late to know—
Thou hast, thou hast found the only way to turn my rage;
Too well thou knowest my jealous soul could never bear
uncertainty. Speak then, and tell me—yet are you silent?
Oh, I am wildered in all passions! But thus my anger melts. 60
(*Weeps*) Here, take this poniard, for my very spirits faint,
and I want strength to hold it, thou hast disarmed my soul.
                                          Gives the dagger

LORD TOUCHWOOD

Amazement shakes me—where will this end?

MASKWELL

So, 'tis well—let your wild fury have a vent; and when you
have temper, tell me.   65

47 *by heaven* Q1 (*om.* W1)
54 *various* changeful
60 *wildered* rendered at a loss how to act or think

52-7 Such 'printing of prose in a form of bastard verse,' in Restoration comedy
quartos, as an 'aid to reconstructing the rhythmic sound of the dialogue,
especially in those more serious passages where emotion takes over,. . .tends to
occur whenever the language of the scene as a whole is approaching the
sentiments or diction of heroic drama' (Holland, p. 112). The dagger crisis has
parallels in *The Rival Queens*, V,i. 124-83, and Otway's *Venice Preserv'd* (1682),
IV, 503-25.

LADY TOUCHWOOD

Now, now, now I am calm, and can hear you.

MASKWELL

(*Aside*) Thanks, my invention; and now I have it for
you.—[*To her*] First tell me what urged you to this violence?
For your passion broke in such imperfect terms, that yet I
am to learn the cause.   70

LADY TOUCHWOOD

My lord himself surprised me with the news, you were to
marry Cynthia—that you had owned your love to him, and
his indulgence would assist you to attain your ends.

CYNTHIA

How, my lord?

LORD TOUCHWOOD

Pray forbear all resentments for a while, and let us hear the   75
rest.

MASKWELL

I grant you in appearance all is true; I seemed consenting to
my lord; nay, transported with the blessing—but could you
think that I, who had been happy in your loved embraces,
could e'er be fond of an inferior slavery?   80

LORD TOUCHWOOD

Ha! Oh poison to my ears! What do I hear?

CYNTHIA

Nay, good my lord, forbear resentment, let us hear it out.

LORD TOUCHWOOD

Yes, I will contain, though I could burst.

MASKWELL

I that had wantoned in the wide circle of your world of love,
could be confined within the puny province of a girl?   85
No—yet though I dote on each last favour more than all the
rest; though I would give a limb for every look you cheaply
throw away on any other object of your love; yet so far I
prize your pleasures o'er my own, that all this seeming plot
that I have laid, has been to gratify your taste, and cheat the   90
world, to prove a faithful rogue to you.

LADY TOUCHWOOD

If this were true—but how can it be?

MASKWELL

I have so contrived, that Mellefont will presently, in the
chaplain's habit, wait for Cynthia in your dressing-room:
but I have put the change upon her, that she may be   95
otherwhere employed—do you procure her night-gown, and

84 *wide* Q1 (rich W1)   96 *night-gown* gown worn as an evening dress

with your hoods tied over your face, meet him in her stead;
you may go privately by the back stairs, and, unperceived,
there you may propose to reinstate him in his uncle's
favour, if he'll comply with your desires; his case is   100
desperate, and I believe he'll yield to any conditions,—if
not, here take this; you may employ it better, than in the
heart of one who is nothing when not yours. *Gives the dagger*

LADY TOUCHWOOD

Thou canst deceive everybody,—nay, thou hast deceived
me; but 'tis as I would wish,—trusty villain! I could   105
worship thee.—

MASKWELL

No more,—it wants but a few minutes of the time; and
Mellefont's love will carry him there before his hour.

LADY TOUCHWOOD

I go, I fly, incomparable Maskwell!   *Exit*

MASKWELL

So, this was a pinch indeed, my invention was upon the   110
rack; and made discovery of her last plot: I hope Cynthia
and my chaplain will be ready, I'll prepare for the
expedition.   *Exit*

CYNTHIA *and* LORD TOUCHWOOD *come forward*

CYNTHIA

Now, my lord?

LORD TOUCHWOOD

Astonishment binds up my rage! Villainy upon villainy!   115
Heavens, what a long track of dark deceit has this
discovered! I am confounded when I look back, and want a
clue to guide me through the various mazes of unheard-of
treachery. My wife! Damnation! My hell!

CYNTHIA

My lord, have patience, and be sensible how great our   120
happiness is, that this discovery was not made too late.

LORD TOUCHWOOD

I thank you, yet it may be still too late, if we don't presently
prevent the execution of their plots;—ha, I'll do't. Where's

97 *hoods* kerchief worn at back of head and draped over shoulders
103 *heart* W1 (death Q1)
107 *it wants* W1 (there want Q1; there wants Q2)
118 *various* turning different ways

---

103 *heart.* This is more concrete and graphic than Q1's 'death.'
107 *it wants.* W1 avoids repetition of 'there,' occuring in the next clause.

Mellefont, my poor injured nephew?—How shall I make
him ample satisfaction?— 125

CYNTHIA

I dare answer for him.

LORD TOUCHWOOD

I do him fresh wrong to question his foregiveness; for I
know him to be all goodness,—yet my wife! Damn
her,—she'll think to meet him in that dressing-room;—was't
not so? And Maskwell will expect you in the chaplain's 130
chamber,—for once, I'll add my plot too,—let us haste to
find out, and inform my nephew; and do you, quickly as
you can, bring all the company into this gallery.—I'll
expose the strumpet, and the villain.   *Exeunt*

[Act V, Scene v]

Enter LORD FROTH *and* SIR PAUL

LORD FROTH

By heavens, I have slept an age,—Sir Paul, what o'clock
is't? Past eight, on my conscience; my lady's is the most
inviting couch; and a slumber there is the prettiest
amusement! But where's all the company?—

SIR PAUL

The company, gadsbud, I don't know, my lord, but here's 5
the strangest revolution, all turned topsy-turvy, as I hope
for Providence.

LORD FROTH

Oh heavens, what's the matter? Where's my wife?

SIR PAUL

All turned topsy-turvy, as sure as a gun.

LORD FROTH

How do you mean? My wife?   10

SIR PAUL

The strangest posture of affairs!

131 *add* Q2 (add to Q1)
  9 *as sure as a gun* most certainly

---

131 *add.* Q1's 'add to' is meaningless.
 11 *posture.* The word recalls 'Aretine's postures' (sexual positions), and perhaps
    also, at the time,
                        Posture Mall,
         The Sexes Harlequin Scaramouche,
         Whose various Scenes of Nakedness are such,
         As e'en makes Nature blush.
    Anon., *The Folly of Love; or an Essay upon Satyr against Women* (1691), p. 13.

LORD FROTH
    What, my wife?
SIR PAUL
    No, no, I mean the family,—your lady's affairs may be in a
    very good posture; I saw her go into the garden with Mr.
    Brisk.   15
LORD FROTH
    How? Where, when, what to do?
SIR PAUL
    I suppose they have been laying their heads together.
LORD FROTH
    How?
SIR PAUL
    Nay, only about poetry, I suppose, my lord; making
    couplets.   20
LORD FROTH
    Couplets!
SIR PAUL
    Oh, here they come.

Enter LADY FROTH, BRISK

BRISK
    My lord, your humble servant; Sir Paul, yours,—the finest
    night!
LADY FROTH
    My dear, Mr. Brisk and I have been star-gazing, I don't
    know how long.   25
SIR PAUL
    Does it not tire your ladyship? Are not you weary with
    looking up?
LADY FROTH
    Oh, no, I love it violently,—my dear, you're melancholy.
LORD FROTH
    No, my dear; I'm but just awake.—
                                                                   30
LADY FROTH
    Snuff some of my spirit of hartshorn.
LORD FROTH
    I've some of my own, thank you, my dear.
LADY FROTH
    Well, I swear, Mr. Brisk, you understood astronomy like an
    old Egyptian.

31 *hartshorn* ammonia-water, i.e. smelling salts

BRISK

Not comparable to your ladyship; you are the very Cynthia   35
of the skies, and queen of stars.

LADY FROTH

That's because I've no light, but what's by reflection from
you, who are the sun.

BRISK

Oh Jesu! Madam, you have eclipsed me quite, let me
perish—I can't answer that.   40

LADY FROTH

No matter,—hark'ee, shall you and I make an almanac
together?

BRISK

With all my soul,—your ladyship has made me the man in't
already, I'm so full of the wounds which you have given.

LADY FROTH

Oh finely taken! I swear now you are even with me, oh   45
Parnassus, you have an infinite deal of wit.

SIR PAUL

So he has, gadsbud, and so has your ladyship.

Enter LADY PLYANT, CARELESS, CYNTHIA

LADY PLYANT

You tell me most surprising things; bless me, who would
ever trust a man? Oh my heart aches for fear they should be
all deceitful alike.   50

CARELESS

You need not fear, madam, you have charms to fix
inconstancy itself.

LADY PLYANT

Oh dear, you make me blush.

LORD FROTH

Come, my dear, shall we take leave of my lord and lady?

CYNTHIA

They'll wait upon your lordship presently.   55

LADY FROTH

Mr. Brisk, my coach shall set you down.
                A great shriek from the corner of the stage

ALL

What's the matter?

35 *comparable* Q1 (comparably W1)
37 *I've* Q1 (I have Q2)
39 *Oh Jesu!* Q1 (*om.* Q2)

35-44 *the very. . .given.* See Longer Notes, No. 5.

LADY TOUCHWOOD *runs out affrighted, my lord*
after her, like a parson

LADY TOUCHWOOD
Oh I'm betrayed.—Save me, help me!

LORD TOUCHWOOD
Now what evasion, strumpet?

LADY TOUCHWOOD
Stand off, let me go, and plagues and curses seize you all!   60
Runs out

LORD TOUCHWOOD
Go, and thy own infamy pursue thee.—You stare as you
were all amazed,—I don't wonder at it,—but too soon you'll
know mine, and that woman's shame.

Enter MELLEFONT *disguised in a parson's habit and pulling in*
MASKWELL

MELLEFONT
Nay, by heaven you shall be seen.—Careless, your
hand.—Do you hold down your head? Yes, I am your   65
chaplain; look in the face of your injured friend; thou
wonder of all falsehood.

LORD TOUCHWOOD
Are you silent, monster?

MELLEFONT
Good heavens! How I believed and loved this man!—Take
him hence, for he's a disease to my sight.   70

LORD TOUCHWOOD
Secure that manifold villain.

CARELESS
Miracle of ingratitude!
They carry out MASKWELL, *who hangs down his head*

---

60 *and plagues. . .all* Q1 (*om.* W1)
60.1 *Runs out* Q1 (*om.* W1)
63.1,2 *disguised. . .*MASKWELL W1 (*lugging in* MASKWELL *from the other side of the
stage,* MELLEFONT *like a parson.* Q1)
71 *villain.* Q1 (villain. *Servants seize him.* W1)
72.1 *They...head* Q1 (*om.* W1)

63.1,2 *disguised. . .*MASKWELL. W1 here has the virtue of elegance.
72.1 *They. . .head.* 'They' presumably means 'servants,' but it is unclear when these
should enter, or lay hold upon Maskwell. Ewald has them come in following
Mellefont. In W1 the direction *'Servants seize him'* is substituted for Q1's S.D.
for the removal of Maskwell, who would apparently remain on stage; see
Introduction, p. xxxvii.

BRISK

   This is all very surprising, let me perish.

LADY FROTH

   You know I told you Saturn looked a little more angry than
   usual.   75

LORD TOUCHWOOD

   We'll think of punishment at leisure, but let me hasten to
   do justice, in rewarding virtue and wronged innocence.—Nephew, I hope I have your pardon, and
   Cynthia's.

MELLEFONT

   We are your lordship's creatures.   80

LORD TOUCHWOOD

   And be each other's comfort; let me join your
   hands:—unwearied nights and wishing days attend you
   both; mutual love, lasting health, and circling joys, tread
   round each happy year of your long lives.

             Let secret villainy from hence be warned;   85
             How e'er in private mischiefs are conceived,
             Torture and shame attend their open birth;
             Like vipers in the womb, base treach'ry lies,
             Still gnawing that, whence first it did arise;
             No sooner born, but the vile parent dies.   90

                            Exeunt omnes

88-90 *Like. . .dies.* 'That the young Vipers force their way through the bowels of
   their Dam, or that the female Viper in the act of generation bites off the head of
   the male, in revenge whereof the young ones eat through the womb and belly of
   the female, is a very ancient tradition' (*Pseudodoxia Epidemica*, in *The Works of
   Sir Thomas Browne*, ed. G. Keynes [2nd edn., 1964], II, 207). Cf. *POAS*,
   V,47-8.

EPILOGUE

Spoken by Mrs. Mountfort

Could poets but foresee how plays would take,
Then they could tell what epilogues to make:
Whether to thank or blame their audience most;
But that late knowledge does much hazard cost,
Till dice are thrown, there's nothing won, nor lost.   5
So till the thief has stol'n, he cannot know
Whether he shall escape the Law, or no.
But poets run much greater hazards far,
Than they who stand their trials at the Bar;
The Law provides a curb for its own fury,   10
And suffers judges to direct the jury.
But in this court, what difference does appear!
For everyone's both judge and jury here;
Nay, and what's worse, an executioner.
All have a right and title to some part,   15
Each choosing that in which he has most art.
The dreadful men of learning all confound,
Unless the fable's good, and moral sound.
The visor-masks, that are in pit and gallery,
Approve, or damn, the repartee and raillery.   20
The lady critics, who are better read,
Enquire if characters are nicely bred;
If the soft things are penned and spoke with grace:
They judge of action too, and time, and place;
In which we do not doubt but they're discerning,   25
For that's a kind of *assignation learning*.
Beaus judge of dress; the witlings judge of songs;
The cuckoldom, of ancient right, to cits belongs.

19 *visor-masks* (a) women incognito (b) whores
26 *assignation* (a) prescription (b) appointment of a particular time and place for a
     rendezvous
28 *cits* citizens, primarily the London tradesmen (an ancient jest)

---

11 *direct the jury.* (a) Concerning the law of the case (b) giving peremptory
     instructions, i.e., that a verdict must be returned for the defendant, or for the
     plaintiff, since there is no case to answer.
17-20 Cf. Horace, *Ars Poetica*, ll. 341-2.

Thus poor poets the favour are denied,
Even to make exceptions, when they're tried.   30
'Tis hard that they must everyone admit;
Methinks I see some faces in the pit,
Which must of consequence be foes to wit.
You who can judge, to sentence may proceed;
But though he cannot write, let him be freed   35
At least from their contempt, who cannot read.

29 *Thus poor poets* Q1 (Poor poets thus W2)
30 *exceptions* (a) pleas made by the defendant in bar of a plaintiff's action (b)
objections made to the rulings of a court in the course of a trial
31 *admit* (includes sense) allow to enter into office (as jurors)
33 *of consequence* as an inference

LONGER NOTES

1. Double-Dealing and Politics, 1690-93

The 'moral' in Lord Touchwood's concluding verses revalues the play as, on one level, a political fable issuing a stern warning to contemporary practisers of 'base treach'ry': Jacobite conspirators, political 'double-dealers,' and false witnesses.

Between 1690 and 1693 England was several times in severe danger from the combination of an invasion from France and a Jacobite insurrection. The real peril ended at the moment it was most acute, in May 1692, with the destruction of much of the French navy at the Battle of La Hogue; but vigorous Jacobite preparations continued during the first half of 1693, until the invasion planned for that summer was cancelled by Louis XIV. Conspiracies continued for two more decades. The active conspirators notoriously included a number of Anglican clergymen (cf. Maskwell's remark that 'there is no plot, private or public, that can expect to prosper without one of [the clergy] have a finger in't'—V,iii. 61-63). A more insidious threat was presented by the unreliability of men who could properly be described as 'double-dealing' in the sense of saying one thing, and doing or intending to do another: men who held positions of trust, including some of the highest offices of state, in William's administration, yet kept up a surreptitious correspondence with the exiled James II, and contacts with his agents, giving fulsome assurances of their support for his cause. Most seem to have been motivated simply by a calculation of their own interests in the eventuality of his recapture of power. James himself complained bitterly of Marlborough's unwillingness to commit himself to any definite action, but 'thought fit to bear with this sort of double-dealing' (J. Dicconson, *Memoirs of the Life of James II*, etc., ed. W.S. Clarke [1816], cited in William Coxe, *Memoirs of the Duke of Marlborough*, etc. [1847-8], I, 32).

Another type of double-dealing, directly comparable to the activities of Maskwell, was the practice of making false discoveries of the treachery of others, in the hope of obtaining rewards for oneself. This trade, pioneered by Titus Oates in the Popish Plot crisis a decade earlier, had two notorious exponents in Thomas Fuller in 1691, and Robert Young in 1692. Young's conspiracy and past career were extensively documented by Thomas Spratt, Bishop of Rochester, in *A Relation of the Late Wicked Contrivance of Stephen Blackhead and Robert Young*, etc., published in two parts in late

1692 (reprinted in *The Harleian Miscellany,* etc. [1800], IV, 198-277). W.H.Van Voris has drawn attention to the similarity between Young, who 'behaved himself with a daring unconcerned confidence, with a bold and erect countenance, though it had naturally very much of a villain in it' (p. 214), and Maskwell, 'a sedate, a thinking villain, whose black blood runs temperately bad' (I,ii. 27-8) (*The Cultivated Stance* [Dublin 1965], pp. 58-9). Spratt's *Relation* may well have influenced Congreve, and supplied several minor hints.

2. The Printing of Q1

The compositors of this quarto, which collates $A^4 a^4 B - L^4$, can be distinguished by their treatment of 'Lord' and 'Lady' in speech-prefixes: A (Ld.,L.) set B1-D4^v, K1-L4^v; B (Ld., Ldy) set E1-F4^v, I1-(part of)I2; C (Lord, Lady) set G1-H4^v, I2(part)-I4^v. The typefaces used in the running-titles change, distinguishing sheets B-D and K-L from sheets E-I.

Five minor press-corrections have been noticed, on a3, C2, F3^v, G4^v and H4^v. The error 'read' for 'reach' on H4^v (IV,iv.72) is at least amusing in its context. The cancellation of leaf G1, because of the original omission of 'go? Won't you' on G1^v (III,i. 557), has been discussed in detail in Fredson Bowers' article, 'The Cancel Leaf in Congreve's "Double Dealer," 1694,' *The Papers of the Bibliographical Society of America*, XLIII (1949), 78-82.

3. III,i. 256: The 'Gulled Bassa'

The Grand Signior many times when he fears the greatness of any *Pashaw,* under colour and pretext of honour, prefers him to the Marriage of his Sister, or some other of his Feminine kindred, by which means, instead of increase of power and glory, he becomes the miserablest slave in the world to the Tyranny and Pride of an insulting Woman. . .[On the marriage-night, when she is ready for] Nuptial Joys: The Bridegroom advised hereof by the nod of the Eunuch, creeps silently into the Bride-chamber, where stripping himself of his upper Garments, he kneels awhile at the feet of the Bed, and then by little and little turning up the Cloaths, gently rubs her feet with his hand and kissing of them, ascends higher to the embraces of his Spouse, which she willingly admits him to, and wishes her self and him a happy Bedding. . .

Sir Paul Rycaut, *The History of the Present State of the Ottoman Empire* (4th edn., 1675), pp. 128, 130. Congreve owned the 5th edition (1682).

4. IV,vi. 47-48: 'Hell has served you even as heaven has done, left you to yourself. You're in a kind of Erasmus' paradise'

Because of Erasmus' reluctance either to support or condemn Luther, the legend grew up that:

> The Papists all so dubious were
> Of his Religion, that i'th'aer
> They hang'd his Corps twixt *Heaven* and *Hell,*
> Knowing not which t'allot him well. . .

'Philanax,' *A Murnival of Knaves, or, Whiggism Plainly Display'd* (1683), p. 29. Also, Erasmus had praised the solitary life as 'a paradise of delights,' in *De Contemptu Mundi* (1489) (*Opera Omnia* [Amsterdam, 1960f.], V:I, 74 [937], 80 [109-110]).

5. V,v. 35-44: Almanacs, etc.

Congreve's exploitation of astrological material in *Love for Love* is here foreshadowed by several allusions to the popular astrology of the almanacs. Brisk's compliment, 'you are the very Cynthia of the skies, and queen of stars,' echoes 'Madam *Cynthia,* Lady of the Night, and Mistress of the Skies, the mutable Moon,' in *Poor Robin 1693, An Almanack of the Old and New Fashion* (1693, sig. C2), within the section dealing with eclipses. Lady Froth's response possibly reflects the insistence that "tis the sun which is the sole fountain of Light. . .the Sun sends Light to the Moon; and she reflects it back on the Earth,' in Bernard Le Bovier de Fontenelle, *A Plurality of Worlds,* transl. J. Glanville, 2nd edn. (1695), p. 38 (1st edn. of translation, 1688). Mention of eclipses leads on to the notion of compiling an almanac (the lady perhaps providing the doggerel verses common in, e.g., *Poor Robin*) and to the man 'full of. . . wounds.' Several contemporary almanacs contain a woodblock diagram of a man, but the version in Henry Coley's *Merlinus Anglicus Junior,* reproduced below from the 1693 issue, seems particularly apt, with its pointers not plain lines but swords, daggers and arrows. Some pre-Civil War almanacs have the man partially dissected. Cf. 'like the Almanack Hero, all over wounds,' Lee, *Caesar Borgia* (1680), dedicatory epistle, ll. 14-15. Brisk's remark utilizes the traditional theory of vision as functioning through the emission of rays from the eyes, which poetically might kill or wound the lover.

The Dominion of the Moon in MAN's Body passing under the Twelve Zodiacal Constellations.
♈ Head and Face.

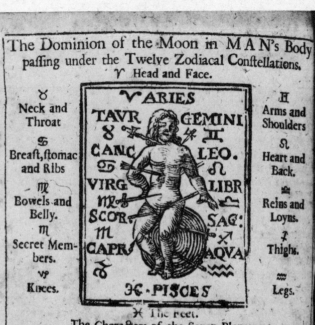

♉ Neck and Throat

♋ Breast, stomac and Ribs

♍ Bowels and Belly.

♏ Secret Members.

♑ Knees.

♊ Arms and Shoulders

♌ Heart and Back.

♎ Reins and Loyns.

♐ Thighs.

♒ Legs.

♓ The Feet.

The Characters of the Seven Planets.
♄ Saturn, ♃ Jupiter, ♂ Mars, ☉ Sol, ♀ Venus, ☿ Mercury, ☽ Luna, ☊ Dragon's Head, ☋ Dragon's Tail.

Upon the Twelve Signs.

♈ Majestick *Aries* clad in's *Golden Wool*,
Commands the Head and Face: The Zodiack's *Bull*
♉ Rules Neck and Throat: The Arms and shoulders lye
♊ Subjected to the Zodiack's *Gemini*:
♋ *Cancer* the Breast and Stomack do obey,
♌ And Regal *Leo* o're the Heart doth sway
His Royal Scepter, whilst the wanton *Maid*
♍ Claimeth the Belly: Reins and Loins are way'd
♎ By the Cœlestial *Libra*: Secrets are
♏ The poisonous *Scorpions*: And the Thighs the share
♐ Of *Sagittarius*: But the Feeble Knees
♑ Fall to the *Goat*: The Legs are standing Fees
♒ Unto *Aquarius*: Whilst the Feet do bend
♓ Their steps to *Pisces*, and assign an END.

These Characters are no Inchanting Tools,

APPENDIX

THE SONGS

The music for the songs was published in *Thesaurus Musicus: being a Collection of the Newest Songs, The Second Book* (1694), from which it is here reproduced.

The songs also appeared separately in folio as *Two Songs from the Double-Dealer*. Printed by J. Heptinstall, for John Hudgebutt. And are to be sold by Jo. Money [1694] (Wing C5877). A copy of this item is reported in the Harvard Library.

In addition to the extensive repetitions, the lyrics exhibit minor differences in words and punctuation (in consistency, in 'Cynthia frowns,' 1.10, Q1's 'does' has been retained, in place of W1's 'must'). Spelling, capitalization and musical notation have been modernized.

(1) 'A Song. . . Sung by Mrs. *Ayliff*, Set by Mr. *Henry Purcell*' (II. 151-162)

Cyn-thia frowns when-e'er I woo her, Yet she's vexed, she's vexed if I___ give o-ver; Much, much_ she fears I should, I should un-do her, But much more, but much more, much

mo — — — — re to lose_ her

lo - ver; Thus, thus in doub-ting she re - fu - ses,

and_ not_ win-ning,_ and_ not_ win-ning,_ thus, thus,

thus she lo - ses; And_ not_ win-ning,_ and_ not_ win-ning,

thus, thus, thus, thus, thus, ___ thus she lo-ses:

Pri-thee Cyn - thia

look_ be - hind you,   Pri-thee

Cyn - thia look_ be - hind you, Age and wrin-kles,

-i-tion; To— be past, be past,———— yet

wish,—— wish,—— wish fru - i - tion, yet

wish,—— wish,—— wish fru - i - tion.

(2) 'A Song set by Mr. *Bowman*. . .' (who as Lord Froth was the singer—III.535-40).

Typeset by Cold Composition Ltd, Tonbridge
Printed in Great Britain by Fakenham Press Ltd, Fakenham, Norfolk